AF334286

From the Tip of My Pen

A Workbook for Writers

Fran Stewart

From the Tip of My Pen

1st edition: © 2009 Fran Stewart
ISBN: 097498765-4

2nd edition © 2010 Fran Stewart
ISGN: 978-0-9818251-6-8

This book was printed in the United States of America.

Library of Congress cataloging applied for

Doggie in the Window Publications
PO Box 1565
Duluth GA 30096
www.DoggieintheWindow.biz

Introduction to the first edition

Four years ago I was sitting next to Adrian Drost at a poetry open mike presentation at Humpus Bumpus Books in Cumming, Georgia. Adrian, for whom English is a second language, leaned over to me between readings and said, "Fran, why don't you write a column for the *E-Quill* to help me make some sense out of this English language?"

The *E-Quill* is the on-line newsletter of the Atlanta Writers Club, to which both Adrian and I belong. *Oh, gosh,* I thought. *Just what I need—one more thing to do each month.* So, in the manner of fine Southern women everywhere (one, after all, does not need to live in the South to have a Southern belle mentality) I said, "Why Adrian, what an idea. I'll have to think about that."

The next day I had an email from George Weinstein, the AWC President, saying, "Adrian tells me you're thinking of writing a column for the *E-Quill*. How wonderful. We'd be delighted to have you on board. The deadline each month is . . ."

So much for my polite refusal. And what a pertinent example of the trouble we can get ourselves into when we don't pay attention to (or don't understand) the nuances of English. Does "thinking about something" imply merely thinking, or is some potential for action (or inaction) automatically involved?

Come to think of it, maybe Adrian was more sly that I thought. Maybe he knew darn well what I meant, and refused to take a vague platitude as a refusal. Hmmm. Wonder what I can rook him into doing for the club?

These thirty-six essays are re-printed just about exactly as they were originally published in the *E-Quill*. I've made a few more minor changes since then (to keep my Inner Editor happy), but I haven't altered the essence. Yes, they are written in a Georgia state of mind. I do, after all, live and work in the South, so you'll find that the end of summer happens in October. I lived in Vermont for twenty-six years, though, so when I write about blizzards, I know what I'm referring to.

Wishing you good reading and good writing always and all ways.

    Fran Stewart
    from my house by a creek
    on the back side of Hog Mountain, Georgia
    September 2006

Author's thoughts about this new volume

For six years now I've been writing a monthly column called *From the Tip of My Pen* for the *EQuill,* the online newsletter of the Atlanta Writers Club. Read the introduction to the first edition to find out how I was convinced (coerced?) into this assignment by Adrian Drost, no mean writer himself. What I'd thought would be a one-year project, though, has built into a truly meaningful part of my month every month.

Three years ago my publisher approached me and asked if I'd be open to having the first thirty-six essays put together in a single volume, to be titled FROM THE TIP OF MY PEN: A MANUAL FOR WRITERS. George Weinstein (who had a part in that initial coercion) wrote a flattering blurb for the cover, calling the book a "Master Class on the craft of writing" and vouching for my "enthusiastic advice." He certainly got that second part right. I have for years been a passionate proponent of the English language in its written forms. In FROM THE TIP OF MY PEN I have tried to convey something of that passion in ways that make it easy for other writers to learn from my experiences.

When it came time to consider a second volume, it made more sense to me to put all six years of columns together for your convenience. If you have the first edition, save it. My publisher will most likely take it out of print, which will make your copy a collector's item, assuming I enter the ranks of the wildly famous. There's no need for you to read the essays in the order in which they were written. A buffet approach works just fine with this book. I think you'll see, though, that my voice has strengthened over the years that I've written these tips.

In preparing this compilation, I thought I'd be revising a lot of the earlier, shorter essays, fleshing them out, finishing them off. I found, though, that—for the most part—they followed my own advice; they were succinct; they were clear; they were fun to read; they gave value. Consider sweet little Essay #29, written for May of 2006. "Inspiration," as it's called, is a mere 191 words; I do believe it's the shortest essay in the entire collection. There are a few others from the early years that round out at 250 or 300 words. As the years have gone on, though, I've gotten wordier.

My Inner Editor wouldn't let me get away without changing a word or two here and there, of course. I've changed the order of some of the essays and even added a couple of complete sentences; yet the overall tone remains as I first wrote these small forays into the amazing complexity, the incredible flexibility, the sheer beauty of the English language.

This second volume is designed as a workbook as well, giving you a chance to spread your wings a bit. The book will not self-destruct if you decide not to accept the assignments. Speaking of which, I debated about the use of the word *assignment* or *exercise,* and decided against it. The suggestions that go along with each essay are an invitation to dance with the tips I've given you. I thought about the term *tip*-dancing, but my publisher ruled against that. Even though they're now called *tips in action,* you can still pull out your tap shoes or ballet slippers or jazz shoes—whatever seems right for you, and watch how taking an active part in the dancing strengthens your writing.

Whether you are a long-time writer or you are just venturing into the field, I hope you'll enjoy and gain value from these essays. They come not only from the tip of my pen, but straight from my heart as well.

  Fran Stewart
  From my house beside a creek
  on the back side of Hog Mountain, Georgia
  February 2010

This book is lovingly dedicated to Nanette Littlestone, who edits my mysteries, stretches me as a writer, and whose friendship has expanded my horizons.

Table of Contents

Table of Contents (continued)

Tips in Action

Work each of these elements into a paragraph:

- the weather
- the political situation of the country
- the time of day
- the setting
- the name of your main character
- the theme of your story
- and finally, its mood.

This may or may not turn out to be a good opening, but regardless of that, it's a great exercise for a writer.

Ah, Beginnings

1

AH! BEGINNINGS . . . How do we begin our short stories, essay, novels, scripts?

One of the best beginnings ever written, to my way of thinking, is the first scene of *Macbeth*, in which the three weird sisters tell us in fewer than a dozen lines, the weather (thunder, lightning, or in rain), the state of the country (when the battle's lost and won), the time of day (ere the set of sun), the setting (upon the heath), the name of the main character (there to meet with Macbeth), the theme of the play (fair is foul, and foul is fair), and finally, the mood (fog and filthy air). Pretty good for eleven lines, eh?

> *I plan to pull out a couple of dozen of my favorite books and look at the first paragraph of each.*

January is a slow month for gardeners, so I always have some extra time now for writing. This month, however, I'm going to spend part of that time examining beginnings. I plan to pull out a couple of dozen of my favorite books and look at the first paragraph of each. What caught me about those first few words? What drew me into the page and made me want to keep reading? I challenge you to do the same exercise. Then, let's all look at our own writings and do some spiffy self-editing on those first few lines. Do those lines move the reader right into the action? Or, at the very least, right into the mood?

Once that's done, just be sure the middle and end of your writing lives up to the promise of that snappy beginning. Piece of cake.

Tips in Action

Go through something you've written recently and highlight every single adverb in the first ten or twenty pages. List them here:

_______________ _______________ _______________ _______________

_______________ _______________ _______________ _______________

_______________ _______________ _______________ _______________

_______________ _______________ _______________ _______________

_______________ _______________ _______________ _______________

_______________ _______________ _______________ _______________

Now shine a bright light on each one of them, as if you're a detective grilling a suspect. *Do I really need you?* Ask that, and be willing to hear the answer—*No*.

<table><tr><td><h1>2</h1></td></tr></table>

Two Much Salt and Pepper – Adverbs

WHAT'S SO WRONG about adverbs? Aren't they perfectly good words? Can't they add a lot of emphasis to our writing? Well, yes. And no.

Editors have been red-lining adverbs right and left for decades, yet some writers still insist on phrases like, *"Just what do you think you're doing in my pantry?" she exclaimed excitedly,* or *I ran hurriedly down the staircase after the gunman,* or *"Slow down, Sally," Buster drawled laconically, "you're almost making me break out in a sweat."*

> **Feel free to use adverbs excessively – in your first draft.**

Now, try each one of those sentences without the adverbs. Incidentally, the first example could do without the stage direction, too. Why do we need *she exclaimed excitedly* when it's obvious from the first two words that she must be upset about something? If, however, you insist on *she exclaimed,* let it stand by itself, or substitute she spit at him / shouted / hollered / grunted / snapped.

In the second example, the act of running *is* hurried, so no adverb is needed. Perhaps, though, instead of running I could have stumbled down the staircase, or maybe I flew / sped / rushed / dashed.

In the third example, drawling is laconic by definition (one cannot drawl quickly), so the adverb adds no useful information. We might not even need to be told that it was Buster who was doing the drawling. If Sally has just been talking, the new paragraph and new quotation marks would indicate that Buster is now the speaker. Do remember that a number of well-loved authors have managed very nicely for years with just an occasional *he said* or *she said* to indicate the speaker's identity.

Does this mean adverbs are never to be used? Well, as William Saffire, that master of language, once noted in an essay called Rules for Writers: "Remember to never split infinitives; passive voice is not to be used; and finally, avoid clichés like the plague." So, feel free to use adverbs excessively – in your first draft. After that, it's a good idea to leave them all out and see if the result is stronger. Adverbs are the salt and pepper of writing; too lavish an application will overpower the prose.

Tips in Action

Take one chapter of your novel. If it's in first person, rewrite it in third person and study how that change affects the mood, the premise, the nuances of the story.

If you've written it in third person, then change it to first.

Now pick a different character and write it in that person's voice. You may or may not decide to rewrite, but I can just about guarantee that this will illuminate some of your weak points (and some of your strong ones).

The "I'd"'s of March: Contractions

ONE OF THE quickest ways to indicate the style of a character is through using, or not using, contractions. Contractions in everyday speech are so common that, as writers, we might forget to make use of the stylistic implications. Consider the following bit of dialogue:

> "Pamela, if you're thinking I'd rather go to the cemetery alone, you're right."
>
> "If you'd like to be safe, Tom, you'd better take me along."

This frequent use of contractions tends to indicate a less formal exchange than the following:

> "Pamela, if you are thinking I would rather go to the cemetery alone, you are right."
>
> "If you would like to be safe, Tom, you had better take me along."

> **The goal is to make your writing understandable and believable.**

This sounds stilted until we replace the names Pamela and Tom with Natasha and Boris. Can you see that not using contractions in dialogue is an effective way to show that the speaker does not (doesn't?) speak American English as a native language? This non-contracted form of speech can also be used if the speaker is non-human, whether it be animal or alien.

A lack of contractions in speech can also indicate that a word is stressed. "If you'd like to be safe, Tom, you had better take me along." Notice how this shift emphasizes the word *better*. Feel free to use a mix-and-match approach to the use of contracted words. The goal is to make your writing understandable and believable.

Although contractions are acceptable in conversation, avoid too many of them in third person narration. First person narration, however, often sounds truer with contractions. Let's look at the same dialogue presented as two types of narration:

<u>Third person</u>: Pamela knew he'd wanted to go alone, but she'd insisted, for only she knew there'd be an ambush, and she couldn't tell him yet. Without contractions, that third person

narration would read: Pamela knew he had wanted to go alone, but she had insisted, for only

she knew there would be an ambush, and she could not tell him yet. This is the form that is generally more acceptable to editors. I'd prefer a mix of the two, leaving in "she'd" and "couldn't."

<u>First person</u> narration, since it is meant to indicate the voice of the character/narrator, can use contractions more acceptably than third person narrative, like this: I knew he'd wanted to go alone, but I was the only one who knew there'd be an ambush, and I couldn't tell him yet. Decide whether your first person narrator is the chatty type (use contractions) or a more formal individual (do not use them).

You have the right and the responsibility, as a writer, to use language effectively. Contractions are a subtle way to impart information. Notice them as you read. As you become aware of how your favorite authors use contractions, you will easily remember to make conscious choices in your own writing.

Tips in Action

Choose a story or a chapter you've written, and redline every unnecessary word. Be ruthless. You can always add them back in, but for now, root out every word you can.

Strive for sentences that are spare to the point of emaciation. Delete all those redlined words and read the result. Now consider the deleted words one at a time. Just as in exercise number two, grill them.

If you had to pay a hundred dollars for every word you write – would you truly think each one was important?

April Showers

EVERYONE KNOWS THAT water dilutes, makes less strong, neutralizes. As writers, we need to strengthen our prose, so those April showers of excess words must be stopped. Let's get out our red pencils and try it on these three examples:

> 1) Martha walked over to the window and stood silently looking out at the cold, icy rain that was falling from the sky.

What would you delete? We know that icy rain is cold; we know the direction rain falls. I might take out the words *over, silently, cold,* and *that was falling from the sky*. And maybe the word *out,* unless I wanted to emphasize her separation from nature. The result? Martha walked to the window and stood looking at the icy rain.

> *By eliminating the excess verbiage, we get a much cleaner sentence.*

> 2) Thomasina patted her own frizzy red hair self-consciously as she gazed, awestruck, at the self-possessed, sleek-haired woman who strode confidently in through the doorway.

By eliminating the excess verbiage, we get a much cleaner sentence: Thomasina patted her own hair as she gazed at the sleek-haired woman who strode through the doorway. A case could be made for various other substitutions, depending on what needed to be emphasized in the story. Perhaps we need to be reminded that her hair is frizzy and/or red, but Thomasina wouldn't be patting her own hair if she weren't self-conscious. The trick is to strip as many words as possible, and then decide, one at a time, whether or not each word is necessary.

> 3) On Saturdays, we would always go for picnics in the park.

"Would" is one of those words that is generally overused. Each Saturday we took food and blankets to the park. Of course, picnics usually take place in parks, as opposed to forests or parking garages, so the words "in the park" could easily be eliminated. Try: Saturdays were picnic days. On Saturdays, we went on picnics. Every Saturday, picnics were the agenda. The possibilities are endless, as you can see.

The point here is to decide what information is pertinent to the story. Leave out all the rest. Readers may enjoy swimming in your flow of words, but they do not need to drown.

Tips in Action

Pick three periods of history that you find intriguing.

Without doing any particular research, simply try to imagine how the people of that time would have spoken. Try writing a simple conversation between, say, a husband and wife, or between two sisters. Use whatever spelling you think is appropriate for that time.

Then, let a trusted friend (someone from your critique group, perhaps?) read the result. Confusing? Ridiculous? Enlightening? Pathetic?

Rewrite it and simply suggest the time period through judicious word-choice rather than through hard-to-decipher dialect.

5

The Merrie Month of May –
Special Effects in Language

YE OLDE CURIOSITY Shoppe would drive most of us nuts if we had to read about it on a regular basis. If you write historical fiction (or fact), remember that the people you are writing about thought, spoke, and reacted in ways that, to them, were modern. An occasional use of the creative spelling we've come to associate with previous centuries may help to create the setting of your piece, but a constant barrage of ye and thee and olde and thither and hence tends to irritate readers; at least it irritates *this* reader. Often the best way to indicate an historical setting is simply to adopt a more formal tone in the narrative and an occasional odd word, phrase, or spelling in dialogue. Pay attention to the use of rhythm in your dialogue. Regional variances in speech often depend as much on the way the words combine to *sing* as they way they're spelled or pronounced.

> *The harder it is to decipher, the less likely your book is to be read. Suggestion is the key.*

The same is true of dialect used in a book of any genre. The harder it is to decipher, the less likely your book is to be read. Again, suggestion is the key. Let the person who records your book on tape or CD be the one to supply the full dialect, for dialect is easier to hear than to read.

Of course, in historical writings, it is just as important to avoid anachronisms, such as having a fifteenth century nobleman quoting Shakespeare, who was born in the mid-sixteenth century. Every detail in historical fiction should be appropriate to the age about which you are writing. A good reference tool is *The New York Public Library Desk Reference*. It has, for instance, a list of Significant Inventions and Technological Advances, which will show you that you can have a character wearing eyeglasses in the year 1350, but not in the year 1250, since spectacles were invented in 1285.

First check your own facts, and then use a good editor to be sure your writing is age-appropriate.

Tips in Action

Look through your recent writing and find one tired, over used word. *Ever, really, easy, happy, suddenly* – these are all good suspects.

Fill this page with variations on that one word; some possibilities will be quite close in meaning, some may range far afield. Some may be one-word substitutes, while some may involve phrases.

Could you use these fresher words in your manuscript?

6

June Bugs to Avoid

COMPUTERS CRASH WHEN there are too many "bugs" in the programs. And our sentences can crash when we inadvertently leave bugs in our writing. Let's look at some quick examples of common bugs that I've collected lately.

<u>Grammatical Errors</u>. I know we often say, "I should of gone to the store," but the correct phrase is "should have gone." If you write "should have," your readers will *hear* "should of" as they read it. If, however, you write "should of," half your readers will think you don't know English. Remember that written English is more formal than spoken English.

> *Feel free to start your own bug collection.*

Can you use "I shoulda gone to the store" to indicate someone who is either not well-educated or is highly casual? Yes, you can, but dialect or non-standard spellings are very tiring when over-used.

<u>Mistakes in Syntax</u>. "I only have eyes for you" sounds perfect as the title of a song, but in written English, it translates as, "I have eyes for you, but my arms are for someone else." In prose, the proper sentence would be, "I have eyes only for you." It may not sing well, but it means what it says.

Syntactical errors often happen, too, with negative sentences, such as "All cats are not Siamese." As it is written, this sentence informs us that there are no Siamese cats in existence. If we wish to state that some cats are Siamese and some are not, we would write, "Not all cats are Siamese." By this token "All that glitters is not gold" would become "Not all that glitters is gold." Some gold, after all, does glitter; so do gold-colored sequins.

<u>The Wrong Words at the Wrong Time</u>. One reason the English language is so rich is its many homonyms and synonyms. Homonyms are words that sound the same, but have different spellings. Examples are words like bee and be; hole and whole; its and it's; there, they're and their. Synonyms are words that sound different but have similar meanings. Please notice that I did not say they have the same meanings. The diversity of English allows us to choose from an almost limitless number of nuances. Take the word *easy*, for example. We could substitute

any of the following words: smooth, facile, simple, effortless, ready, comfortable, gradual, tolerant, or gullible. Although they each have distinct shades of meaning, they all mean easy—more or less. Good writers choose the word that most closely conveys the desired meaning.

Feel free to start your own bug collection. I hope, though, that the bugs come from writings other than your own.

Tips in Action

What are the dilemmas in your life?

List four and write at least one sentence (or even one paragraph) about the repercussions of each: *if I do this, such and such could happen; if I do that, so and so will be affected in this way.*

- If I do this, ____

  If I do that, ____

- If I do this, ____

  If I do that, ____

- If I do this, ____

  If I do that, ____

- If I do this, ____

  If I do that, ____

7

Word Puzzles

BEFORE THE DECLARATION of Independence was created, the Founding Fathers of this country found themselves in a dilemma. They longed for freedom from what they saw as the oppression of the king, but they feared the repercussions of an open revolt. At the same time, each of them had specific beliefs about how the new entity they wanted to form should be set up, and they feared that they would be unable to effect a government that would work not only in the 18th century, but that would continue to function through the following years.

> *Whether or not to cook oatmeal for breakfast when one loves oatmeal but one's spouse detests oatmeal, is not a dilemma.*

They had not just one problem (how to gain freedom without retaliation), but two. They were faced with the second difficulty of forming a government if and when they were successful in their revolt against the king's might. Even if they had success in their first venture, there was a chance that the second would end in failure. Even if we revolt and win, will we ultimately fail?

Other than the fact that this is the month of July, what does this have to do with writing? It's the use of the word *dilemma.* This is an example of a word that has come to be used by many writers in a fuzzy cloud of guesswork. Whether or not to cook oatmeal for breakfast when one loves oatmeal but one's spouse detests oatmeal, is not a dilemma. It is perhaps a problem, a puzzle, a quandary, or even a predicament. It does not have that essential quality, though, of having to choose between two (or more) possible outcomes, either of which may be dangerous, or at the very least disadvantageous.

Another case in which the fine shades of meaning are frequently ignored is the use of the word *mentor* instead of *teacher.* A mentor is someone who may very well be a teacher, but who goes beyond the usual scope of teaching. When you use the word *mentor* in your writing, you are implying that the person is a trusted guide or counselor. If you want a different word than *teacher,* try *coach* or *tutor, instructor* or *guru,* or even *educator.*

I suggest a good dictionary as a staple desk accessory for every writer. Even the simplest word in English generally has many possible alternatives. Your job as a writer is to find the right one to use. This is not a dilemma; it is simply a puzzle—a matter of doing your homework and knowing the true meaning of each word you choose.

Tips in Action

Choose a recent event and write a cogent paragraph about it as if you were reporting it right after it happened.

Now add fifty years to your time frame and write another paragraph. What will you have to explain so that your children or grandchildren will understand it?

Next add two hundred years, and see what happens.

Care to write a book now about time travel?

8

Hot Topics

IN WRITING FICTION, a story can be greatly enhanced, and made to seem much more believable, by inserting references to actual events of the time period about which one is writing. In historical fiction, this is easier to do, since we know what events have lasted in the public memory. We know, for instance, that most readers will understand what we're referring to when we mention the signing of the Constitution or the use of the guillotine by French revolutionaries.

> **What seems a hot topic for today simply may not stand the test of time.**

The waters become more hazardous, though, when we write fiction about more contemporary times. It may be tempting to set the stage by throwing in comments about the latest music craze or a raging political argument. If those situations eventually become common cultural knowledge, then your story will seem richer to future readers. If, however, they are simply passing fancies, then readers even a decade from now won't be as likely to understand what you were talking about. Instead of building a rich background for your story, you may simply be rendering it outdated or confusing.

What seems a hot topic for today simply may not stand the test of time. How do you make the choice, then? It's a matter of judgment. I don't know of a definitive way to tell what will last and what will fade. If you choose to pepper your contemporary fiction with current events, you might want to explain them. Instead of simply giving the name of a rock band, for instance, show your main character reacting to the music. Is it loud, dreamy, obnoxious, R-rated, ear-shattering, crooning, politically-motivated, sensual, or heavy on the electric guitar? Have your character comment (or cringe or yelp or coo or go into a trance). That way you will inform readers, current and future, just what is going on in this hot topic of the time.

Tips in Action

Self-editing is difficult for some people and down-right impossible for others, yet it is a helpful tool indeed. Try it with something you've written recently.

Truly examine each sentence. Try reading a paragraph backwards, word by word, in order to see the spelling of each word. For instance, read this:

backwards pargraph a reading Try .sentence each examine Truly .recently written you've something with it Try

Did you spot the misspelling in this example?

School Days

DID YOU EVER have an English teacher who insisted that you learn how to diagram sentences? What on earth was the value of that torture? And do we have to know how to diagram a sentence in order to construct decent, readable prose?

It depends, I suppose, on who you ask. Mrs. Van Aken, my senior English teacher at Mascoutah High School, told us that Hemingway could break all the rules because he knew very well what they were to begin with. If we know from diagramming what is a subject and what is a predicate – or so the argument goes – we will be less likely to leave one out. Hmmm. Depends on what the end result is supposed to be. The use of incomplete sentences (such as the last one you just read) may often be effective. As a writer, though, be sure you know why you are breaking the rule.

> *Hemingway could break all the rules because he knew very well what they were to begin with.*

In an industry that relies on agents and editors, it makes sense to misuse standard English usage and grammar only when there is a good literary justification for doing so. Why risk having your manuscript red-lined or simply rejected by someone who thinks you've made multiple mistakes? Judicious proof-reading can transform a mediocre manuscript into a work of art. Get someone who's truly picky to do the proof-reading for you. Ask that person to highlight every single grammatical error. It can be illuminating to see how many times you begin your sentences with the word *But* or *And*.

"But, that's the way my character talks," you object.

Is it the way your character truly would talk? Or is it simply the way you've been used to writing ever since you forgot how to diagram a sentence?

Tips in Action

Look for groups of three in your own writing and test them for that singsong rhythm. If "oh my" is suggested by the cadence, rewrite them. If you can't find any examples in your own work, put these into sentences:

- apples and oranges and limes ________________________________

____

____

- pencils, erasers, and pens ________________________________

____

____

- hurricanes, earthquakes, and floods ________________________________

____

____

Three-Word Horror Shows

I saw the Ghosties, and Goblins and Freaks.
We counted the Aces and Deuces and Treys.
They cleaned their Pistols and Rifles and Knives.

MANY WRITERS USE groups of three, simply because it can be an effective way to increase the tension of a phrase. Feel free to use such groups in your writing, but be aware of the *Rule of Threesomes* (as opposed to the oft-quoted *Rule of Three*). And what, you ask, is the *Rule of Threesomes*? It says that if you group three items together, you risk sounding like Dorothy and her friends in *The Wizard of Oz*. This all depends on the number of syllables in each item. Try reading the three examples above out loud. Try to do it without adding "Oh my!" at the end of each phrase. Hard to do, isn't it? Think of "Lions and tigers and bears. Oh my!"

> *How can you use your list of three items without losing your readers?*

Now, how can you use your list of three items without losing your readers? Rearrange the words, so they don't have that sing-song rhythm. Change or replace some of the words if necessary. Like this:

> I chose to walk outside on Halloween in spite of all the freaks and ghosts and goblins.

> We knew some cards were missing, but in order to prove it, we had to count the cards in every single deck, every ace, every deuce, every trey.

> The D-Squad was ready. They had spent the morning hours cleaning their pistols, oiling their rifles, and shining their knives.

In 1910 Edwin Arlington Robinson wrote a poem called *Miniver Cheevy*. It is full of threesomes, well-worded and never boring. Here's one verse that has two threesomes in it:
> *Miniver sighed for what was not,*
> *And dreamed, and rested from his labors.*

He dreamed of Thebes and Camelot,
And Priam's neighbors.

One of the later verses goes like this:

Miniver scorned the gold he sought,
But sore annoyed was he without it.
Miniver thought, and thought, and thought,
And thought about it.

This shows a different way of dealing with a group of three: make it a foursome.

Go ahead. Sharpen your pencils, scribble out some threesomes, and enjoy reading them. That's right: Sharpen and Scribble and Read. Oh my!

Tips in Action

Mark every single point of view in a chapter you've written. Remember that sometimes those POV shifts can be subtle.

The question to ask yourself is whose head am I in right now? Check it over sentence by sentence. If you find yourself waffling in and out of various characters' brains, diligently rewrite the entire paragraph (or chapter) from only one point of view. Then rewrite that entire selection from someone else's POV.

Compare the two and decide which is stronger.

Points of View (A and B)

"I don't much like Thanksgiving," said the turkey.

The lioness dragged the antelope past the sleeping male.
"King of the jungle?" she thought. "Ha!"

"Hurray! It's a new record!" Timmy Turtle cheered as his best friend
crossed the finish line.

NOVEMBER IS THE month when we concentrate, presumably, on gratitude. Writers have many reasons to be grateful. We can, after all, do what we love (write) at our own pace (midnight to 2:30 anyone?) wherever we happen to be (now where did I put that scrap of paper?) It would behoove us though (I always wanted a reason to use that word) to consider spicing up our prose (or our poetry) by using unusual points of view. Thanksgiving, for instance, from the viewpoint of the turkey.

> *This is the blinkin' BIRD talking!!!*

Remember that the key phrase for a writer is *What if*. . . What if the lioness, who does all the hunting, refused to feed the male? What if the turtles applied to the Olympics? The people in your stories, books, or poems often will gain interest when they are not predictable. They can still be believable without being boringly conventional. This is not to say that you should have little old ladies routinely joining circuses. But, why not have *one* little old lady do so?

There is another aspect of *point of view* that a writer should keep in mind. I once wrote what I considered to be a delightful little paragraph telling what a bird would have seen if she had been looking at the (human) character I was describing. "The little finch sitting on the tree overlooking the pathway," I wrote, "could have made twelve nests in the pockets of the utilitarian vest the hiker wore . . ." and so on. It sounded perfectly fine to me. My editor thought otherwise. "No, no, no," she red-inked, "you may not think like a bird when you are describing like a person." How could I have used the image without distorting the point of view? *He tried to reach into one of the dozen or so pockets that covered his hiker's vest. "Drat it!" he muttered. "These pockets aren't big enough to make a finch nest in."* Okay, I admit this may be a bit forced, but do you get the idea?

When we jump from one point of view to another, we must give the reader a clue as to what we are doing. This is usually done by leaving a blank line in the text, but it is considerably more effective if we rewrite to a consistent point of view. While we are speaking of Melinda's thoughts as she stands in line, we cannot switch to telling what the salesclerk is thinking. We might, however, mention that Melinda could see a furrow forming between the eyebrows of the harried clerk. This is still from Melinda's point of view, yet it gives information about the clerk – or rather about Melinda's interpretation of what she saw.

It can be enlightening to take a piece of your own prose and mark up the margins with *Tammy's point of view; Miranda's POV; Tom's vantage point; This is the blinkin' BIRD talking!!!* It can also be a humbling experience.

Tips in Action

If a resolution for a whole year seems insurmountable, take heart. Make a "writing priority" list for one week (or one day, or even one hour, if that seems more achievable). Write it down here.

After one week / day / hour, write a paragraph or two about what you accomplished and how you feel about it.

New Year's Resolutions for Writers

1. I will write nothing but scintillating prose, if I can figure out how.

2. I will avoid clichés like the plague.

3. I will maintain a consistent point of view at all times. She thinks she can do this?

4. I will use spell check. Eye will knot trust spill chick.

5. I will buy useful reference books. I will use them.

6. I will write every day.

7. I will not compare myself to published writers (such as Sue Grafton who wrote this rule).

8. I will encourage other writers.

9. I will ask opinions only of people whose opinions I trust.

10. I will read. I will learn from my reading.

11. I will laugh when I think I have writer's block. Laughter opens the valves.

12. I will make index cards for my characters. I will therefore recall who has black hair and who has blond.

13. I will keep a list of these resolutions and will resolve them again next year.

> *I will keep a list of these resolutions and will resolve them again next year.*

Tips in Action

Choose a page or two that you've written and underline or highlight every adjective. List them on this page.

Study the list. Can you justify each one? If not, why not? (Bland, ordinary, overused, excessive . . .) Delete those. If you find one you feel you can justify, describe how it adds to the strength of your story.

13

Snow Storms and Avalanches

I HAVE A friend, who will remain blessedly unnamed for this column, who peppers his (unpublished) writings with a veritable blizzard of adjectives. Three potential side effects of blizzards—I know this because I lived in Vermont for twenty-six years—are as follows:

1. People can get lost in blizzards.
2. Blizzards can make people feel cold.
3. Too much snow at one time can turn into an avalanche.

It has always seemed to me that too many adjectives (that is to say, more than one or two per sentence) imply that the writer believes in a certain stupidity on the part of the reader. I don't write for dense people. My target audience is well-read. Therefore, if I shower them with flurries of excess words, they will not feel well-informed so much as bored silly. Where is the adventure in reading if the author has spelled it all out in excruciating detail?

> *This is not the picture of a happy guy doing a little recreational yard work.*

Let's look at this example:

Marjorie, feeling bored and lonely, turned her long-lashed emerald-green eyes downward. She inspected the curve of her long, bright red, tapered fingernails. One had a wide heavy scratch that crossed the nail as if a big angry tiger had taken a vicious swat at her. She ignored the domineering and somewhat intimidating Arthur, even though he continued to pace like a hungry lion in front of her chair. He no longer had any hold on her empty and devastated heart.

Now let's try it without any adjectives at all:

Marjorie turned her eyes downward. She inspected the curve of her fingernails. One had a scratch that crossed the nail as if a tiger had taken a swat at her. She ignored Arthur, even though he continued to pace like a lion in front of her chair. He no longer had any hold on her heart.

I would probably put back in the word *hungry*, but that is the only adjective necessary in this paragraph. You might opt to put in *emerald* or *long*. This is where good editing, which simply means good choosing, comes into play. While I doubt you got lost in the blizzard of the first example, I'd bet that you found it hard to care what the heck Marjorie thought about anything. There was simply too much nit-picky information about her. In the second section, though, a reader has a chance to ask, "Why is she looking downward? Don't hopeful people generally look upward?" Do you recall the first lines of Edwin Markham's poem *The Man with the Hoe*? He talks about a man *bowed with the weight of centuries* who leans on his hoe and gazes at the ground. This is not the picture of a happy guy doing a little recreational yard work. Would we have learned more about the man if Markham had said he was discouraged, illiterate, tired, worn-out, exhausted? Of course, Markham goes on to use a number of adjectives – it *is* poetry after all. But that first word-picture of him looking down sets the premise of the poem.

An essential element of prose is the careful choice of the exact detail that is necessary to further the action of the chapter, the story, the novel. Even poetry can be over-adjectified. Before you write another line, toss all your adjectives onto a compost heap of words. Once they've cooked down a bit, you can pull out what's left one at a time. Remember to use no more than one simple little lonely modifying word per fascinating, scintillating sentence. Whoops! I mean *one adjective per sentence, please.*

Tips in Action

Sketch a rough skeleton on this page. Don't worry about your artistic abilities. You know the foot bones will be at the bottom and the skull at the top.

Now look through a chapter you've written. Decide what it's based on. That's the label that goes by the feet. Where does the action come in? Label the legs. The bones of the hands and arms might be the twists and turns in the story. The spine is the description of either the setting or the characters. The shoulders would be the problems encountered by the protagonist (carrying the weight of the world on one's shoulders).The skull would be the resolution of the chapter.

So, now you should know how your chapter is built and how it got that way.

14

Cutting Down Trees

A NEIGHBOR OF mine is in the process of clear-cutting his property. It doesn't seem to matter to him that he bought a house in the middle of a forest. He's decided to cut down every blinkin' tree on the place. He does not get my vote for the best tree-editor on the back side of Hog Mountain. His delete-saw is working overtime, and his judgment seems to have eroded (along with his hillside) into the creek that separates our back yards.

Most self-editors do not have his problem. We tend not to cut out enough. Of course not. Our words are precious to us. Aren't they our babies? Didn't we linger over the choice of them? If we've struggled to put 75,000 words on paper, why would we want to delete thousands of them? Haven't I mentioned this very same thing in several other *Tip of My Pen* articles? Well, yes. You see, it's important.

> *His judgment seems to have eroded (along with his hillside) into the creek that separates our back yards.*

I encourage you to write all you want to — every adjective, every adverb, every single word you feel like writing. I then encourage you to use your chain saw, better known as the delete key, without compassion on every hackneyed phrase, each unnecessary character, and all those confusing scenes that didn't ring true in the first place. Now, see what you have left. Are the bones of your story holding together without all that excess verbiage? Remember, if a story line is good, it doesn't need propping up. If it's bad, all the propping in the world won't disguise its poor quality.

The good news about all this paring down is that we can put it back in if our (paid) editor says something miraculous like, "This section is too much like a skeleton. It needs some fleshing out." At that point, you'll probably go back and put in better words, better descriptions, better characters.

I wish my neighbor could put back those trees that used to measure two feet in diameter.

Tips in Action

For this one you may need to travel to the library. Or you might simply walk to a nearby bookcase. Pull out a favorite book and find a page of dialogue.

- What type of language style was used?

- How long were the sentences?

- How much supporting verbiage (he said, she said, he commented, she asked) was necessary?

- Now ask those same questions of something that you've written and compare the answers.

- Is your dialogue in any way memorable?

- If not, try rewriting it as if it were in that favorite book of yours.

- What did you learn, and how can you apply this to whatever you write from here on out?

15

A Different Drum

I BOUGHT MYSELF a birthday present in January. It's the *Simon & Schuster Super Crossword Puzzle Dictionary & Reference Book.* I happen to believe that every writer should play around with well-crafted crossword puzzles, just because doing so helps sharpen our vocabulary. And we all need to know the name of a South African fox, or the rivers that pass through Switzerland, don't we?

When we find a believable bit of conversation in a book, we can stop to analyze why it makes such an impact on us.

While browsing through the book, though, I found lists of Pulitzer Prize Winners from 1917 on. Here is fodder indeed for us to ruminate on in order to improve our writing skills. I'm not talking about copying another writer's style (not that we could do it anyway). I *am* talking about broadening our scope of experience with ways of telling a story. How do other writers deal with dialogue, for instance. When we find a believable bit of conversation in a book, we can stop to analyze why it makes such an impact on us. What type of language style was used? How long were the sentences? How much supporting verbiage (he said, she said, he commented, she asked) was necessary?

Now my *To Read* list is a great deal longer than it was a week ago. But I'll be reading winners, and I bet I learn a lot from them. I'll still walk to my own drumbeat. I'll still write with my own distinct voice. But there will be echoes. Oh yes. There will be echoes.

Tips in Action

I'm not going to ask you to list your challenges here. We all hear way too much of the negative every day. Look at what is good about your writing and the way you do it, your life and the way you live it.

Ten advantages to being the kind of writer I am	How I can put those advantages to use

16

Paying Taxes

THERE ARE A lot of people who are convinced that taxes, like death, are inevitable. Then there are the so-called immortalists, who believe we ought to be able to kick the death habit. I don't, however, hear any of those folks preaching about eliminating taxes. We pay these ubiquitous taxes in many forms, sales tax, property tax, income tax, and those special-use taxes that we get a chance to vote on every couple of years.

What are the taxes a writer pays, though? Keep in mind, I'm not talking about money here. Hopefully we're making enough of that from our writing that we can pay the government its share. I'm talking about the non-governmental things that tax a writer.

> *Instead of feeling taxed by the chores that seem to pile up around me, I'm going to come to terms with my inner slob.*

Most writers I know work out of their own homes. Unless we can figure out a way to separate our work time from our home-time, there is grave danger that all the home chores will call us away from our pen and paper (or computer and keyboard). Ditto the family's needs. Being interrupted by a toddler or called upon by a spouse who needs an extra pair of hands tends to tax our creative time. Of course, we always have the choice of ignoring the dryer that is beeping every five minutes, but that incessant reminder can drain our attention away from our writing. Sure, we can jump up, do another round of our chores, and hit the keyboard again. But how many ideas can we lose in the process of shifting gears like that?

On the other hand, how many people working in sterile offices would relish a chance to juggle chores and work throughout the day? What other profession would allow us to play at what we love doing – and call it work? I've decided to shift my thinking. Instead of feeling taxed by the chores that seem to pile up around me (I have to clean my desk off; I need to finish washing the dishes) I'm going to come to terms with my inner slob. I choose no longer to be taxed by those chores. If I am writing, I will write, until I'm ready to take a break and do whatever seems necessary for me to do. Obviously, if I had small children at home, those necessary moments would be more frequent, and my writing would get jammed into naptime or after-bedtime segments. There is, after all, such a thing as priorities. But I will no longer consider children/pets/chores a taxing element. I will pay them as necessary. And, between times of paying my taxes joyfully, I will play (excuse me, I meant to say work) at my writing.

Tips in Action

Five things I want to DO:

Five things I want to BE:

Five things I want to HAVE:

17

Maybe or Maybe Not

HAVE YOU EVER heard about a Do-Be-Have List? This is one of the most powerful tools in my toolbox of ideas, and I'd like to share it with you this month. I have so many people ask me, *how did you do it? How did you get your murder mysteries published?* And I have to tell them that the most important step was the first one, deciding that I truly wanted my books published. 'Yeah, right,' I can hear you saying. Give me a moment to explain.

I've wanted to be a published author for dozens of years. But that wanting usually took the form of idle, wishful thinking. One day, several years ago, I took a workshop of some sort and learned about keeping a Do-Be-Have List. Here's how to do it, and then I'll tell you why it works. Take three sheets of paper (or you can do it on the computer, of course). Label the first one *100 things I want to do*. Then, start listing those things. This is not the time for self-censorship. You don't think you'll ever get a chance to go rafting down the Colorado River? So what? Put it down anyway. Write *go scuba diving in Hawaii* even if you can't swim yet. Or *climb Mt. Washington* even if you get out of breath walking to the mailbox. *Go on a walking tour of Greece, learn to speak French, make friends with my next door neighbor, learn to play the harmonica, be with my dad when he dies.* You get the idea. Keep listing everything you can think of that you wish you could do. If you want to be a published author, put down something like *see my books on the best-sellers list*. Another good one is *win the Pulitzer.* Now go to the second page.

> **This is about making a personal statement of commitment that says–notice the capital letters– THIS IS WHAT I WANT.**

Head it: *100 things I want to be*. Even if you've never shared a bit of your writing with anyone, you might want to head the list with *I want to be a published writer. I want to be a Pulitzer Prize-winner.* Keep going, listing all those things you want to be. Think ten years old. My niece at ten wanted to be a firefighter, a police officer, a teacher, a doctor, and a nurse. All of them. Oh, and a marine biologist, too. Whatever you think you want to be, write it down. *Author of (fill in the name of the book you want to write)*, for instance.

Okay, you're doing well. Now, *100 things I want to have*. Hot tub, a creek in my back yard, a deciduous forest around my house, a maple sideboard for my dining room (glass windows

in the top where I can display my published books!), skylights, a bay window where I eat breakfast, lots of climbing posts for my cats, a loveseat for the living room, a wood-burning stove in the fireplace. Keep going.

I can pretty much guarantee you won't get to 100 on any of these lists right away. But keep adding to them as you think of other things. And check them off one at a time as you accomplish them. I date mine, by the way. You see, we as writers know that writing is a powerful tool. So, why don't we use it to move our lives to higher planes of accomplishment? This system works because when we write down what we want, we give a strenuous message to our subconscious. Reviewing the lists from time to time will help keep those ideas percolating. And you will be more likely to see the opportunities for accomplishment as they come up. Would you remember all those things you wanted if you didn't have them written down? Maybe. Maybe not. This is not about forgetting or remembering. This is about making a personal statement of commitment that says–notice the capital letters–THIS IS WHAT I WANT. That message is hard to ignore.

I don't share my lists with anyone, by the way. I don't want people to laugh at me when they read that I'd like to learn to play a tuba some day. But I just finished eating breakfast next to my bay window, looking out at the creek which runs through the forest of deciduous trees in my back yard. And while I was eating I could smile at my published murder mysteries displayed behind the glass windows of my antique hardrock maple sideboard, as the sun streamed in through the skylight above me. I don't have that hot tub yet. But it's on my list, and I'm pretty sure it's going to show up some day.

Do. Be. Have. Maybe it's worth a try.

Tips in Action

Find a conversation or a particularly important descriptive passage in your novel or story. Parse out how the syllables would read.

To do this, follow my examples and write the sentences using CAPS to indicate the accented syllables. See if you can find a regular rhythm. If so, does it back up what you're trying to imply in that passage? Peace, anger, boredom, resentment, contentment, rage.

Try rewriting to develop a more effective rhythm. Many writers, of course, do this subconsciously, but if you're trying to improve your writing, an exercise such as this one can be enlightening.

Do you almost always write in one particular rhythm? Again, the answer will be good to know.

18

Oklahoma!

THE REVIEWS OF the new musical were atrocious. They predicted it would fold early. I seem to remember having read somewhere that one well-known reviewer wrote: *no legs, no jokes, no chance.* He was talking about *Oklahoma!* That exclamation point, by the way, is a part of the title. I, the original exclamation-point-deleter, did not put it in there to get you excited about my prose. Think about that title song, though. Wouldn't we all love to write something as memorable? Something that would capture the imagination of our readers. The perfect novel, short story, screenplay, poem that would have folks quoting it for generations to come.

> *Without those distinctive rhythms, our writing just won't sing.*

With that thought in mind, think again about the song. Is it the words you remember or the melody? I'd be willing to bet it's the melody you recall. In a song, it's the music that lasts. The words may be delightful or poignant or simply exuberant, but unless the music itself works its way into our hearts, the song won't last. Since this column is about words, though, how do we as writers come up with the equivalent of a melody?

We use the rhythm of words, varying the rhythm to change the tone. June is a good time to think about sunshine, so let's look at some examples of how the subtle shifting of rhythms in a basic informational sentence can convey different shades of meaning. Here we have a person in a rowboat. She is looking at water dripping from the oars.

1. The sparkling sun as it dripped from the oars transported Lynne to a space of deep contentment.

2. Sunlight, cutting through the water, bounced off every droplet. Lynne was blinded for a moment.

3. "Sunshine?" Lynn quipped. "You think I'm impressed with *sunshine?*"

4. Lynne wanted to say to him, "The funny thing about water is that it's so . . . so liquid. See how the sun shimmers right through it? See how each droplet glows?" A shadow struck his eyes. She couldn't speak. The moment passed.

Okay, let's think about these. I'll re-write them with the stressed syllables in all caps.

1. The first example trips along with a three-syllable rhythm:

    the SPARK-l-ing SUN as it DRIPPED from the OARS - - TRANS-port-ed LYNNE to a . . .

    At the very end, though, we are forced to slow down as the rhythm changes so that we can join Lynn in her SPACE of DEEP con-TENT-ment.

2. The second example is completely unforgiving in its stark one-two, one-two rhythm.

    SUN-light, CUT-ting THROUGH the WA-ter, BOUNCED off EV-ery DROP-let. LYNNE was BLIND-ed FOR a MO-ment.

3. Number three starts with a number of stressed syllables in a row. This rhythm lends credence to sarcasm.

    SUN-SHINE? LYNNE QUIPPED. YOU think I'M im-PRESSED with SUN_ SHINE?

4. The first half of the fourth example has multiple shifting rhythms, that seem to reflect Lynne's feelings about the water.

Lynne WANT-ed to SAY to him, "The FUN-ny thing about WA-ter is that it's SO . . . SO LI-quid. SEE how the SUN SHIM-mers right THROUGH it? SEE how each DROP-let GLOWS?"

The second half of that section, though, reverts to a one-two rhythm that stalks along and helps us to understand, at a subliminal level, why Lynne is unable to voice her thoughts. A SHA-dow STRUCK his EYES. She COULD-n't SPEAK. The MO-ment PASSED.

In singing, it is the melody that lingers. In writing, it is also the melody, the rhythm that carries our readers along and makes our writing memorable. Of course, little things like plot and characterization help, too. But without those distinctive rhythms, our writing just won't sing.

Tips in Action

The next time you get stuck, write a paragraph about one of the following ideas:

- *popcorn*
- *rattlesnakes*
- *plastic bottles*
- *a photograph in your wallet (or on your desk)*
- *a one-hundred-dollar bill with a phone number on it*
- *face paint for a clown*
- *a flat tire*
- *termites*
- *a badly-written poem*
- *file folders.*

Now, just keep writing.

19

Heat

Stultifying. Don't you love that word? It means a lot of different things, but I'm referring to the sense of reducing one to the point of futility. That's what too much heat tends to do to me in July and August and September. I still need to write, though. I simply can't justify taking off one-fourth of the year.

So, how do I overcome the stultifying effect of this heat, without simply turning down the thermostat on the air conditioner? (I dislike freezing as much as burning up.) I have two sure-fire remedies. First, I pay attention to deadlines. Deadlines cause action, despite the heat, despite the stupor of my brain, despite my longing to sink into a cool mud puddle (if I could find one) and keep the hogs company. I can carp all I want about writer's block and lack of inspiration and a paucity of ideas. But when push comes to shove (yes, I've even devolved into using clichés, as you can see), a looming deadline awakens a faint spark of life in most writers' minds.

> *A looming deadline awakens a faint spark of life in most writers' minds.*

The funny thing is that once I sit down and start putting words on paper, the blocks seem to dissolve. Oh, I often throw out the first three or four things I write – I self-edit like crazy – but the simple act of writing stirs a writer's blood. This is, after all, *what we do.*

So here's my tip of the month for dealing with the stultification of mid-summer. When the heat of a deadline is on, pick up your pen and put the tip of it to the paper. The ideas may start as simply a dribble, but pretty soon they'll be flowing enough for you to swim in. I can just about guarantee it.

And, the second sure-fire idea? Drink more water. It keeps the blood in your brain from congealing. How's that for a scientific reason?

Tips in Action

Think about the book you're writing as a series of layers. You can imagine that each chapter is a separate layer. What order do you want to put those in?

List the chapters on separate index cards with a brief summary of what happens in each chapter. Now lay them out in order as you've written them. Shift them around and think about the ramifications to your story.

What if this happens before and that happens afterward?

20

Compost

I SPENT TODAY helping a friend of mine build a two-section compost bin. In the process, I learned a lot about the way my mind works. Last night I sat down with a pencil and a paper napkin and sketched out the top and side views, so I'd know how I wanted it to go together, how many 2 x 6s we'd need, and where the nails went. This morning, although I started by looking at my sketch, I realized that I didn't need it. The compost bin was already built inside my head. I could *see* the finished product.

As a writer, I'd like to say that the process of writing is just as simple. Sketch out the general plot, list the characters, figure out their motivations, and *see* the finished result. Then simply write it. Right? Wrong.

> **The compost bin was already built inside my head. I could see the finished product.**

The vital difference between a compost bin made of wood and wire and nails, and a novel made of paper and ink is that the people in the story have a way of hopping up from the outline and heading off into strange tangents, rather as if one were building with living kudzu that keeps springing new leaves or growing three feet before the next nail goes in. In YELLOW AS LEGAL PADS, my last book, I'd written three-fourths of it before I even knew who the dead body was. Unlike wood and nails, the kudzu-like characters have a way of surprising us.

When we build a compost pile, we need to layer green stuff (like grass clippings and cucumber peels) with brown stuff (like dead leaves, dirt, and coffee grounds). Then the earthworms go to work and the chemical action of decomposition heats up the pile. The result is amazingly fertile soil. In our books, we need the brown stuff which is the nitty-gritty work, the sketchy outline, the effort of putting it all down on paper. But we also need the green ideas, the twists of plot as our characters surprise us. Then, when the earthworms get to work digesting (rewriting) the whole mess, it somehow turns into the rich soil we were looking for in the first place.

Today, as you are writing, try imagining the compost pile you're building. Build those layers. And don't forget the earthworms.

Tips in Action

Just for the fun of it, play around with some unusual words. Open a dictionary at random and find five or six unfamiliar words.

As a writing exercise, build a paragraph around those words. You can be silly if you want to, or approach this as if it were vital to the survival of the human race. Either approach will work. Just use your creativity, your inventiveness to write an intelligible few sentences.

When we stretch ourselves as writers, we grow.

21

Pools

POOLS OF WORDS – try using the words *cursoriness, perspicacity*, and *numinous* in valid sentences. Now try using them in a way that sounds natural. The English language is filled with words of rich and varied meanings, and those shades of meaning can shape our prose, adding dimension and depth to the written page. When we dip into the pool of words available to us, though, we need to be sure we are not likely to drown in it. It's great fun to try out unusual words; see if they can bring a spark of life to an otherwise dreary sentence. Such words are generally more acceptable in poetry than in prose (although Peter Wimsey could get away with a fair number of them. Of course, Peter had Dorothy Sayers as his creator, and Harriet Vane——no mean vocabularist herself—as his love. And then again, Sayers wrote at a time when the working vocabulary of the average reader was something like 33% higher than it is today.). In poetry, *numinous* might just fit the bill. In prose, *spiritual* or *mysterious* wins out almost every time, no matter how much I might like poor little *numinous*.

> *Sayers wrote at a time when the working vocabulary of the average reader was something like 33% higher than it is today.*

Please note that I am not suggesting that writing should be sprinkled with sesquipedalian words (ones that are a foot and a half long) or with arcane references that impel a reader toward a dictionary or, more likely, toward the TV set. Unusual words, used simply for the sake of their rarity, turn our writing into a freak show. A well-chosen term, however, that gives the precise shade of meaning we're trying to convey, can illumine a dark and otherwise dingy corner of our prose.

I must admit that I'm someone who reads the dictionary for the fun of it, happily filling the void left by my not having a TV set. I'd like to think, however, that I have enough discrimination not to be lured into writing that "Biscuit McKee felt a need for cursoriness," when it would make much more sense to say "she was in a hurry," or that "her perspicacity surprised her husband." Why not just say he couldn't believe she'd figured *that* out?

The deep pool of a dictionary or thesaurus is a fearsome enticement to writers who don't know how to swim around the tantalizing temptations that could pull us into a whirlpool of

self-aggrandizing verbiage. (See what I mean?) Please note: we'd be the only ones to drown there, because our readers would have bailed out a long time ago. Let's give those readers the benefit of assuming they are intelligent and discerning people, who have a dictionary close at hand if they need it. But let's not throw them into needing it on every single page. We don't, after all, want to join that pool of writers who are deservedly ignored.

Tips in Action

Go ahead. I dare you.

Pick up a pencil and a few sheets of paper.

Head outside and settle yourself under a tree or on a deck, at a playground or next to a lake, in a park or on your front steps, and see how your writing blossoms.

22

Pencils

WE DID IT! We lived through another summer. I may have thought I'd never stop wilting when I walked out into that wall of humidity that lurked outside my door, but—lo and behold—it's coming up on autumn and my windows are open again.

This is a good time to take up where I left off last spring and begin to write outdoors. Even if you have a laptop, why not try stepping outside and writing with a pencil, just for the fun of it? It's a truly marvelous invention, and it's been around since 1565. Anything that's lasted that long must have a few things going for it.

Let's see . . .

> *It's a truly marvelous invention, and it's been around since 1565.*

1. It's portable.

2. Runs without batteries. For that matter, it can run without brains, but I hope that's not the case here.

3. Has an eraser, the 1565 version of a delete key.

4. Provides a handy canvas for tooth imprints. I've never known anyone who hasn't occasionally chewed on a pencil. What computer gives a frustrated writer that kind of alleviation? I don't group solitaire, Pac-Man, or minesweeper in the same league with a yellow number 2 Ticonderoga.

5. Can be thrown across the path / room / deck when simple deletion or chewing is not active enough (see numbers 3 and 4 above).

6. Can be sharpened without a fancy gadget. My Swiss Army knife works just fine. In a pinch I can even sacrifice a fingernail to tear the wood back away from the graphite.

7. Can be broken in half to fit in a tiny notebook or a small pocket. Of course, this eliminates the delete function of one-half of it, but I can use the bare half for my *Journal of Work in Progress*. That *Journal* isn't edited, after all. It just gets me rolling and gives me a chance to air those vague ideas. And the just plain stupid ones that will never show up in my finished manuscript, but need to be released from my psyche before the good ideas can roll out.

Go ahead. I dare you. Try writing outside, under a tree or on a deck or next to a lake, and see how your writing blossoms. And all because of a simple pencil.

Tips in Action

Pick a particular event you tend to ruminate about.

Now, instead of trying to turn your brain off, write that scene twelve different ways. Be sure the outcomes vary wildly.

Include one that spells success, one that invites disaster, one with tears, one with smiles. Try out rage; then try on meekness.

23

A Cow's Life

SOMEONE RECENTLY ASKED me if I had any thoughts about the creative process. What writer hasn't? I would quibble a bit with the word *process* in that question, though, for *process* sounds so tidy. I'm pretty sure the creative impulse that leads to writing must be shored up, for each individual writer, with a veritable toolbox of individual habits and techniques. Put together, the tools in that toolbox may look like a rather motley assortment, but if they help the writer create, then they are worth far more than their proverbial weight in gold.

Ruminating, for instance, is a tool frequently found in almost any writer's toolbox. Like cows, who cannot digest grass quickly (who could?), but need to chew their cuds for hours at a time, writers often take an unwieldy idea and chew away at it from a dozen different angles until it begins to soften, and the nutritious juice that must have been there all along begins to ooze out.

> *Writers often take an unwieldy idea and chew away at it from a dozen different angles until it begins to soften.*

I love ruminating. As I'm driving to the post office, I can take a mundane conversation that happened four years ago, and reinvent it twelve different ways. In one my companion becomes agitated, in another she wilts with discouragement. I may have her throw herself off a moving train, or I may have her save me from dashing in front of a taxi to pursue a bank robber. In my writer's mind, I can do anything, go anywhere. If I don't like where I've gone, I just regurgitate the scene and rewrite it. Fun? You bet!

As we think about creativity in general, I challenge you to jot down your ideas about it in your constant companion—the notebook you depend on. Ah! A notebook, another of those tools that aid the creative process. Some of the ideas in *my* notebook . . . okay I admit it . . . *many* of the ideas in my notebook would take an unconscionable amount of regurgitation and chewing to amount to anything. But once in a while there is a glimmer of useable material. So I take it out and chew, and chew, and chew, and chew. Then, when my ruminating is far advanced, I write and write and write.

I've been known to read what I've written to the squirrel who spends an inordinate amount of time running up and down the tree outside my office window. But the squirrel as inspiration (or audience) is another topic altogether. This column, I'll read to the cows.

Tips in Action

Why do frogs always have to walk, hop, or swim?

Because their cars keep getting toad.

Now, you tell one.

Resolutions, Again

LAST YEAR AT this time, I came up with a list of what I considered to be quite reasonable resolutions. Resolutions for writers, that is. In the past year, I've pulled out that list occasionally and reflected, as writers will do, on it. This year is a re-write, called for by my Inner Editor. Here they are:

- I will write nothing but scintillating prose, if I can figure out how.

  > Oh, nonsense. Scintillating prose gets old fast if that's all there is. Good old short Anglo-Saxon words and simple straightforward sentences have a lot to be said for them. Forget the *scintillate* and go for *sense*.

- I will avoid clichés like the plague.

  > I've managed to use a few in my books, usually between quotation marks, coming out of the mouths of characters who tend to think in clichés. I'm going to relax and allow a few here and there.

> *Good old short Anglo-Saxon words and simple straightforward sentences have a lot to be said for them.*

- I will maintain a consistent point of view at all times. She thinks she can do this?

  > This I do only because my editor redlines POV's when I'm not consistent. I get away with it by hitting *enter* twice and getting into someone else's head. Where there's a will, there's a way (see cliché resolution above).

- I will use spell check. Eye will knot trust spill chick. – This one stays as is.

- I will buy useful reference books. I will use them. – So does this one.

- I will write every day.

  > Nope. Some days I will think a lot, or do other things like buying groceries. Some days I will allow myself the time to nurture myself with a healthful marvelous massage. And then I will go into a long spell where I write every day, all day long and half the night, and thoroughly enjoy it.

- I will not compare myself to published writers (such as Sue Grafton who wrote this rule).

Yes, I will. I will compare like crazy, and I will learn from their strengths. I will also learn from what I perceive to be their mistakes. I will, however, never get discouraged by those comparisons.

- I will encourage other writers. – Yes.

- I will ask opinions only of people whose opinions I trust. – Yes.

- I will read. I will learn from my reading. – Yes.

- I will laugh when I think I have writer's block. Laughter opens the valves. – Big fat YES.

- I will make index cards for my characters. I will therefore recall who has black hair and who has blond.

  This year, I will remember to look at those index cards.

- I will keep a list of these resolutions and will resolve them again next year.

  Or revise them as necessary. I love rewriting!

Tips in Action

Choose something you've written recently and underline or highlight all the "polyester" words.

Now, what are you willing to do about this? Would you . . .

- Take a class?

- Read a how-to book?

- Join a critique group?

- Attend a writers club meeting?

- Hire an editor?

- Find a mentor?

- Consider a complete rewrite?

- Do a partial rewrite?

Knitted with Love

FOR THE PAST several months I've been knitting helmet-liners out of 100% wool yarn. This is part of a nation-wide project for knitters to help the troops stay warmer overseas in the winter. The problem these are meant to solve is that the polyester helmet-liners provided by the government simply don't keep *anything* warm.

There's probably nothing wrong with synthetic fibers other than the fact that they're made with petroleum, aren't they? And they don't stop the cold. And they don't feel particularly comforting. And they're not made with love by those machines that sew them.

> *Why settle for polyester words?*

What does this have to do with writers? Lots. Let's be sure that when we knit our stories, our poems, our essays, we do it with love and with the very best materials we can lay our hands on. Why settle for polyester words when we have dictionaries, thesauruses, great workshops, and the legacy of our English teachers at our disposal? Why settle for polyester, poorly-knit plots when with a little extra care (okay – a *lot* of extra care) we can weave, knit, or crochet the very best creations we are capable of? Why let our readers freeze their way through an unsatisfactory story line, when, with 100% commitment, we can warm their hearts and fire their imaginations?

Let's decide to write only with 100% wool for the whole rest of the year. Or in the summer, we can switch to 100% silk. It's the 100% that matters. As long as it's not 100% polyester.

Tips in Action

Isn't it obvious what this assignment will be?

Choose an issue about which you feel some passion. Argue for it. Then argue against it.

Put those arguments in writing. Don't cheat, either; truly play the devil's advocate for the side you've already decided against.

Cats & Dogs

YEARS AGO, I read about a political science professor who assigned his students the task of listing 100 reasons why capitalism was good for our economy. When they came back to him with their lists in hand, he told them to write 100 reasons why capitalism was ruining our economy.

That particular exercise might not impress us unless we happen to be writing articles about inflation or recession. The concept, though, of looking at each issue from multiple sides, is an enlightening one for writers. Take cats and dogs, for instance. If you're a dog person, you already know why dogs are wondrous creatures. You know their many benefits – their soul-felt love, their single-minded devotion, their sheer exuberance. Other than pooper-scoopers, though, have you thought about the down-side of the story? No fair asking cat people to fill you in, as I'm sure they could. The cat people need to be making their own list, about the advantages of dogs.

> *If you're a dog person, you already know why dogs are wondrous creatures.*

"Why?" you ask.

I'll tell you. As writers, it behooves us (*love* that word!) to flex our imagination, and what better way than to argue, Socratically, for the *other* side? When we question our own opinions, it becomes easier for us to draw life-like characters who are unlike ourselves. The trouble, now, is that I'm going to have to follow my own advice and put a dog person or two in my murder mysteries. But first I'll need to make up a list. When we understand our fictional characters, they become multi-dimensional. We are no longer satisfied with drawing them as stick-figures on a flat canvas.

Why would you even want to write a person whose psyche was completely hidden from you into your novel or short story? How can you write convincingly about a person who is a vegetarian unless you know all the reasons that could be motivating that character? Just think about it: you might even learn to like rutabagas.

Tips in Action

Pick a journalist whose writing you've enjoyed. It can be someone who has a regular column in a local paper or somebody who is known nationally.

Write that person a thank-you note expressing what you have gained from reading those columns.

Send it.

Headlines and Headaches

I'VE SPENT MORE hours than I care to count at the Loving Touch Animal Care Center in Stone Mountain over the past three weeks. Not that I don't enjoy seeing the fine folks there. I was delighted a number of years ago to have discovered this holistic vet clinic. They usually show up in the acknowledgment section of my murder mysteries because they answer (seriously!) questions like *How many mice will a cat eat in one day?* or *What's a major injury that a cat can survive and recover from quickly?*

What I don't enjoy is the situation that sent me there. One of my bigger cats injured one of my smaller cats. Poor little Jazzminka was trying to be the peacemaker. She stepped between two of the big males who had been having a tiff of some sort. Panther was just crouching there wishing Harley would quit bugging him. But Harley, contrary to his usual mode of action, had gone on full-scale alert–the code red of the animal kingdom. As I rounded the corner to see what the hissing was about, Jazzminka brushed her head against Harley's left whiskers, and he attacked her. I now have a much better idea of why hockey players can become brutal in the middle of a match, or how soldiers in the heat of battle can kill other human beings. Harley at that moment did not know that Jazz was his buddy–someone he'd grown up with–someone he normally shared a food bowl with and curled up with nose to tail on the yellow-flowered comforter. His deadly instincts blinded him to the reality of little Jazz.

> *I now have a much better idea of why hockey players can become brutal in the middle of a match.*

My point–and there *is* a point to this, is that journalists, the folks who write the headlines, must have a hard time deciding how to present a story about atrocities. We are inundated with those stories. How do we as readers decide whether the journalists are writing responsibly (reporting) or simply fanning the flames of national or international anger? And, if we were the ones writing those news stories, would we choose to dwell on the sensational aspects, or would we be willing to go behind the headlines to find out *why* an incident happened, not to excuse it–for there is no excuse for such incidents–but to explain it with the hopes that the information we present will educate and will prevent future misuse of power.

If you've read this column for any length of time, you'll know I'm a fan of Public Radio. I like the journalism I hear each day on their (deservedly) award-winning news programs.

I like hearing the stories behind the stories. I like hearing news instead of sound-bites. Yes, many of us write fiction, but to those of you who deal in non-fiction, either current or historical, I applaud your integrity when you go to great lengths to report fairly, to record the sometimes difficult events that we need to hear about. I'm sure making those hard choices each day can lead to a lot of headaches, but I for one appreciate your efforts.

And Jazzminka is healing nicely.

Tips in Action

This is an easy one: list some of your favorite but seldom-used words.

Over the next week, see if you can invent a chance to use them in conversation or in writing.

Twilight

I'VE ALWAYS WANTED to use the word *crepuscular* in one of my books, but I've never written any book for which that word would be appropriate. That's part of the problem of being a word collector. There are a lot more words than there are places to use them.

Or, perhaps, part of the problem of too many words is the dearth (there's another good one) of vocabularic expectations in our schools, in advertising, in the media. I doubt *vocabularic* would pass any sort of dictionary search, but you can see what I mean, can't you? Pull out a copy of any book by Dickens; flip through *Moby Dick*; haul out Austen or Alcott or Emerson or practically anything written before 1950, and compare it to *USA Today*, the evening news, or the latest issue of almost any other magazine.

> *We seem to want the easy word more than the precise word.*

Now, I'm not one to go around bad-mouthing the media. We—meaning the general public as reflected in print—seem to want the easy word more than the precise word. We have, as a nation, been willing to give up precision in our language. That distresses me, until 1 discover that I've been comparing the apples of books to the oranges of magazines. Maybe we need the dessert-like lightness, the jazzy contemporaneous simple prose of magazines. But, please, let's keep writing books that give our readers some meat to chew on. Even if not one single *crepuscular* moment shows up in any of them.

Tips in Action

What do you do to lift yourself up again when you're discouraged? List five or six ideas that work the best for you, then refer to the list the next time you wonder how you can possibly keep writing.

29

Inspiration

"TAKE A BREATH, *dear*," is excellent advice for writers. The whole idea of breathing, of oxygenating the cells, is that our cells work better when they are aerated. And brain cells are particularly prone to a need for oxygen. Inspiration, therefore, is more than simply reading or listening to other fine writers and learning from them, being inspired by them. It's a matter of that big inhalation that says, "Wow; I can learn from this."

At last month's meeting of the Atlanta Writers Club, AWC President George Weinstein asked us, "What do you do to overcome discouragement?" I felt a little silly saying, "I breathe." So I didn't say it. I should have, though. That is what I do. I take a few very deep breaths. And then I take a few more. "Breathing sure beats the alternative." Who said that? When I am discouraged, though, I tend to stop breathing or to breathe in a shallow, non-productive manner. Three deep slow breaths, though, will often turn my crummy attitude around.

> *I take a few very deep breaths. And then I take a few more.*

When I'm breathing I can write. And as long as I'm writing—look out world, magic is on the way.

Tips in Action

Check a chapter of your own for any words that end in –ing.

For the purposes of this exercise, you can ignore the word sing. Rewrite the sentences to get a clearer, more succinct expression.

Participles and Pilot Lights

Did you ever have one of those gas heaters that tended to go out on winter nights? If you're as old as I am, you probably did. I can remember my mother clumping her way out of her bed and crouching in the hallway, where I could see her shivering as I peeked over my blue blanket. I was naturally unwilling to get up and help unless she asked me directly.

Sometimes participles are a bit like gas heaters. They do a fine job until they act up. Of course, they act up because we as writers tend to overuse them. A participle, as you know, is a verb-form used as an adjective. Participles often end in *–ing*. Here are a few florid examples:

> *Participles are a bit like gas heaters. They do a fine job until they act up.*

1. His writing style was heavily dependent on flowing words of dubious origin, coming as they did from the intuiting side of his brain.

2. Her dancing partner always left her tapping feet wanting something else—rhythm, for instance, rhythm that should have been the calling card of their cha-cha troupe.

3. They couldn't agree on whether the coming storm held freezing snow or pelting rain, and after bargaining about the pressing need for evacuation, decided to bring out the playing cards and sit tight.

I'm not saying these are grammatically incorrect. They're not. Can you see, though, that a paragraph full of such statements becomes like a heater whose pilot light is always going out? Just when we expect a good terse descriptive word, we get a waterfall of *ing*'s. Try these, instead:

a. He borrowed unknown words, and used them with little grace.

b. Whenever she danced, her cha-cha partner spoiled the rhythm.

c. They couldn't predict the weather, so they played cards instead.

These sentences are tighter, clearer, more to the point than the first three were. The fact that they avoid participles helps in that clarity. Not every participle needs to be replaced, of

course, but a whole string of them weakens any sentence. If you write about someone who gives *a running commentary in the driving rain*, consider changing it to *he rambled on while we got soaked*. Choose your words, all of them, with care. Then they'll keep you warm on a winter night.

Tips in Action

Ask published friends who their editors are. Ask them what their experience has been with the editing process. Research an editor sometime before the end of this week. Try to find out:

- Does this editor work on your type of manuscript? Some editors may work only on non-fiction, for instance.

- What are the standard charges?

- Would the editor be willing to edit one chapter, so you can tell if it's a good fit?

What an Editor Isn't

1. An editor isn't your mother. When Joyce Carole Oates spoke at Vermont's Trinity College in the 1990's, she told us that every time her mother read a manuscript she would say, "Joyce, this is the best thing you've ever written." We may enjoy such gushing indiscriminate approval from someone, but that someone should not be our editor.

2. An editor isn't your best friend who was an English major and who can tell you when your commas are misplaced. Punctuation and grammar need to be checked. We need to know if we tend to start sentences with the word *And* or the word *But.* Proofreading, however, is not the same as editing.

> *We may have to cry a bit before we recognize the value of the editor's feedback.*

3. An editor isn't a psychopath who kills your manuscript regularly and viciously. There is a difference between someone who is brutally frank and someone who is frankly brutal. A good editor can ask you to delete a character or re-write an entire chapter without attacking your value as a writer or your status as a functional human being.

For a pre-published (read *eternally hopeful*) writer, finding an editor before submitting to an agent is a wise step on the writing career path. We are so sure of that polished manuscript of ours—until we place it in the hands of a good editor. We may have to cry a bit (I certainly have occasionally) before we recognize the value of the editor's feedback, but our manuscript then goes to the agent in its best possible form. Of course, once it's sold to a major publishing house, *that* editor asks you to refine it further. By then, though, you will be an old hand at this business of turning your baby over to the professionals and trusting their judgment.

First, give it to your mother. Then let your English major friend read it. Avoid the psychopath. Find an editor.

Tips in Action

Take a chapter (or even one reasonable-sized paragraph) that you've written and do three re-writes:

- chatty / home-town style

- hard-boiled / nitty-gritty style

- philosophical / erudite style

Decide:

- Which do I like best?

- Which do I like least?

- And why?

Mockingbirds, Crickets, and Humpback Whales: A Writer's Voice

ALMOST ANY SCIENTIST can tell you that when you record animal sounds and slow them way down, the resulting music is intricate, involved, intriguing. Each sound is also unique to that individual species and to the animal itself. That's what *voice* is. That's what we as writers strive to reach—our own distinctive way of imparting the stories we tell.

A valuable exercise for any writer is to take a passage, any passage, and try to give it different voices, each distinct from the others. Let's say, just for the fun of it, that you're describing a tree.

> You might want to use words that bring to mind the windswept, stark landscape of *Wuthering Heights*.

> Perhaps *Moby Dick* comes to mind. I know, I know. There weren't any trees on the ocean. But that sense of man grappling with overpowering natural forces could lend itself to your vision of the tree as a vindictive presence, rather the way Tolkien did with Old Man Willow in *The Hobbit*.

> A Hemingway tree would be terse.

> An Austen tree would be proper but would have a mind of its own. Get the idea?

That's what we as writers strive to reach—our own distinctive way of imparting the stories we tell.

Then, let's borrow from the animals in the title. The trouble with mockingbirds is that they don't have a distinctive voice of their own, since they're so good at borrowing voices from everybody else. So we might want to avoid too much "mockingbird" in our descriptions. Crickets, on the other hand, have that unimaginably involved chirruping. It may sound simply like background noise in the woods at night, but record it and slow it down, and you have a veritable symphony. The good news is that you get to choose, as a writer, which aspects of the cricket chirp you want to emulate. Ditto with whale songs. Do you go for the high squeaks or the resonant bass soundings?

Of course, regardless of which author or which animal you admire, your own voice, after you've done all your experimenting, must be uniquely yours. It is only when we step into our *voice*, pulled from the sum total of our life experiences, that we become full-fledged writers. Cheep, chirp, chatter; squeak, hum, or boom. You decide.

Tips in Action

Take your latest manuscript—novel, story, poem. Sketch a map of the territory it encompasses. Think about how well you know the setting you're trying to evoke.

33

Maps

THINK ABOUT MAPS. Think about the way they lay out a town, a countryside, a nation, in tidy grids. Highways, rivers, mountains. Or perhaps, neighborhoods, stores, parks.

Now think about your own writing. Do you have a map in your head? Do you *know* where your characters live? Not just the name of the city or town or state, but the lay of the land. Can you translate that map onto the page? Do you know how long it takes to get from point A to point B, say from Mortimer's apartment to Angelina's classroom? Could you sketch the relative relationships of *this* house to *that* building? Do you convey that sense of space to your readers?

I tend to like books that have maps in the front of them, but I'm willing to forgo the map if the author can *show* me the town, or enough of it so that I can see where the action is. *Next door* in a subdivision of townhouses is going to have a different feel than the *next door* of a rural community, a country club development, or a slum. A block is a widely variable term, depending on whether you're talking city, country, mountainside village, or seaside resort.

> *A block is a widely variable term, depending on whether you're talking city, country, mountainside town, or seaside resort.*

Don't tell me Mortimer *walked three blocks* to pick up Angelina from school (and, by the way, is she the teacher, the student, the guidance counselor? Is this high school, grade school, college? Is he her father, her boyfriend, her parole officer?) Show me the trees along the way, show him striding across vacant lots. Does he dodge traffic in his haste? Or does he stroll by the bakery and stop in to pick up croissants and wine for a celebratory picnic?

Draw me a map, a map with words, so I can feel I'm a part of your journey. And if you pick up croissants, give me a call. I love picnics.

Tips in Action

Read *The Elements of Style*. Write your impressions as you go.

34

Strunk & White's Elements of Style

You've never read *The Elements of Style*? You call yourself a writer? Well, I suppose that's a possibility, but why would any writer, or aspiring writer, wish to pass up **the** classic how-to book of all times?

Half the fun of reading Strunk and White (and it *is* fun indeed) is mulling over the examples for the various rules they set forth. One can never forget the difference between the noun *alternative* and the adjective *alternate* after reading, "As the flooded road left them no alternative, they took the alternate route" (p. 40). Clear? Yes. Concise? Yes. We already know, even without reading the definitions, that there is a sense of choice implied with the word *alternative*.

> *It is still fresh, vibrant, and exceedingly useful.*

I compose these columns because three years ago someone for whom English is a second language asked me to write a few tips each month that would help him deal with American English. The point is, though, that we all can use tips about this complex, extraordinary language of ours. The little book known as *The Elements of Style* was first written in 1919. It is still fresh, vibrant, and exceedingly useful. Although it has needed a few modest updates over the nine decades since it appeared as a college text for Professor Strunk's own classes, it still rings with a clarion call for precision.

Five sections. Eighty-five pages. Buy it. Read it. Follow it.

Tips in Action

Sit for a few moments and think about the pace of your own day:

- Are you spinning your wheels, trying to multitask, ignoring human connection because of all your *duties*?

- Or are you so laid back you're practically comatose half the time?

- Is this due to a physical condition, an emotional barrier you've devised, or a preconceived belief about your own abilities?

- How does your schedule affect your writing time?

- What can you do about it?

- What are you willing to do about it?

- *Those last two truly are separate questions.*

35

Thankfulness – Put in Some Breathing Space

I AM RELUCTANT to talk too much about Thanksgiving. We do not have a mandate that says, "Simply because it is November, we must discuss Pilgrims." Thankfulness, though, is another matter altogether, particularly for writers. We want our ideal reader to be thankful that we have written, thankful that we managed to get it published and available, thankful that we have written well.

It's simply not fair, though, to wear out your reader. You may have dozens of high-action scenes crying out to be written into your book. You may have worked and reworked those scenes to keep the suspense at fever pitch.

> *That was when the magic happened.*

Wait.

One of my favorite memories is of the Big Apple Circus that I saw years ago in Vermont. There was a lithe but muscular fellow in jeans, chaps, and a cowboy hat, who spun around the ring twirling a lasso faster than a rope could possibly have been designed to travel. There was an element of fire, although I don't recall exactly what was burning or what he did with it. I do, however, remember the exhaustion I felt. At that moment, with the masterful timing of true showmanship, the cowboy took his bow.

And that was when the magic happened. After several seconds of silence, a single spotlight went up into the audience and illuminated a clown on the top row of the bleachers. He was blowing bubbles and watching them drift across the heads of the audience. We heaved a collective sigh of relief. Suspense is fun. Excitement has its place. The need to breathe, though, is paramount. Because of the clown and the bubbles, we appreciated the exhilaration of the trapeze act that followed.

Let your readers breathe. Between your action scenes, tuck in a moment of contemplation. By giving your readers a slight rest, you can keep them turning the pages. You can keep them thankful for you and your writing.

Tips in Action

Write your ideal holiday meal. Write where it will occur. Put the people who count around your table (or at your picnic blanket, or on your boat, or whatever you've devised).

Write one comment by one of those people. Answer it. Listen to who speaks up next. See where the discussion leads you.

36

Resolutions for the Third Time

TWO YEARS AGO I wrote resolutions in December. Last year I revised them. This year I think I'll ditch the resolutions and talk about spaghetti. Not exactly your usual holiday fare.

More than a dozen years ago, for reasons we won't go into right now, I went through a major depressive phase of my life. One of the symptoms was a complete inability to plan even the most rudimentary of menus. I ended up, for weeks in a row, feeding my family spaghetti every evening. Not a pretty picture at all. When they actively rebelled, I switched to macaroni. And I cut up green onions to put in the store-bought sauce.

Yes, I finally did get much needed help. And I swore, when I started writing murder mysteries, that I would never let my books turn into spaghetti for every meal. Formula writing, with plotting that is so predictable the reader hardly has to finish the book, is the bane of every series writer. The best way to avoid formulaic writing, I think, is to create characters that grow and learn and make mistakes (just not the same ones in each book). Look at the action sequence in your first book. Does your detective argue with her fiancé, trust the wrong person, walk into a potentially compromising situation, find herself in a life-and-death situation as a result, shoot somebody, reunite with her fiancé? Does she then follow this sequence in every single book in the series? If the answer is yes, get yourself a better editor. Even if you have green onions in there, and macaroni, your readers will know it's pasta once again.

> *Even if you have green onions in there, and maca-roni, your readers will know it's pasta once again.*

You could, however, have your detective travel to Italy and eat spaghetti as a holiday meal. Then it's not the same old routine. It's fresh. It's appetizing. It's something new.

Tips in Action

For a day or two, jot down the times you find your-self or your friends speaking in present tense.

Spend a while thinking about it.

Does present tense seem to be an effective method of communication for your purposes? How have you used it in writing? If you use it a lot, try re-writing to see if the meaning will be clarified by some judicious use of past tense or past perfect.

37

Was/Had Been/Is – the Evolution of English

AMERICAN ENGLISH HAS changed without our being aware of it. Language always evolves, with the addition of new words as new technologies come into their own, as musical forms or pop cultural icons rise or wane in popularity.

This change, though, seems more basic to me than the simple addition of words. We seem to have forgotten what it was to remember the past. I'd noticed the change in newspaper quotations, in magazine interviews, and in the conversations of people around me. But it all came to an explosive awareness recently when I heard a Public Radio commentator—that's right, National Public Radio, that bastion of proper speech and erudite ideas—say, "So here I am walking down the street yesterday, and . . ."

> *For decades, I've had a personal vendetta against the Smurfs.*

Whatever happened to past tense? *There I was yesterday, walking down the street.* The street experience happened yesterday, so wouldn't past tense be appropriate in reporting it? Apparently not. Perhaps it's a generational thang, as they say in country music. More and more, I find that people tend to think in present tense, speak in present tense, and write in that same tense. The use of the present tense is so ubiquitous now, that I've experimented with mentioning it to writers with whom I've been speaking, calling their attention to their own use of the present tense, only to be met with incredulous denials. "I don't do that," they say. "Do I?"

For decades, I've had a personal vendetta against the Smurfs, who taught an entire generation that the use of an exact word was never necessary when one could simply use *smurf* as a verb, a noun, any part of speech. Now, I don't consider this move to expressing oneself almost exclusively in present tense to be nearly as insidious as the dumbing down of our language by the little blue critters (or rather, by their script writers). It does give me pause though, to wonder whatever will happen to a handy little word like *had*. As every writer knows, or should know, when we write in past tense, if we have to go even farther back in time, we stick in a *had* (or two) to make the timing clear. After that, we can dispense with the auxiliary word. Here's an example:

> Gladiola Grim played the piano at every social function. We hated it. Her sense of rhythm had always been atrocious, but the last time I heard her play, just before she was murdered, she exceeded our lowest expectations when she executed her variations on *Moonlight Sonata*. I use the term *executed* judiciously, of course, since poor Beethoven would have gleefully strangled her if the stranger wearing a black cape hadn't obliged shortly after the musical fiasco.

There is no need, as you can see, to put another *had* before the word *exceeded*. The timing is perfectly clear. Without the past tenses and past perfects, though, the chronology becomes harder to follow:

> Gladiola Grim plays the piano at every social function. We hate it. Her sense of rhythm is atrocious, but the last time I'm listening to her play, just before she's murdered, she exceeds our lowest expectations when she executes her variations on *Moonlight Sonata*. I use the term *executes* judiciously, of course. Poor Beethoven misses out on strangling her because the stranger wearing a black cape beats him to it.

I would like to keep *had* in the running. If English has to evolve—and what language doesn't?—I'd vote for clarity rather than what I see as a lazy approach to tenses.

Tips in Action

Look for alliteration in something you've written. Can't find any?

Do a quick rewrite on a sentence or two or three to see what you can come up with.

38

To B or Not To B – Alliteration in Language

1. "Whether 'tis better in the mind to suffer / the slings and arrows of outrageous fortune…"

2. "I have a faint, cold fear thrills through my veins / that almost freezes out the heat of life."

3. Better buy the barber a beer before he buries his brother.

4. "Keening. That's what it's doing," she said, cupping her chin in her cold hands, as if she could curtail her fear of the wind by keeping her teeth from chattering.

> *See how effectively one can set the stage by echoing subtle sounds.*

IT PAYS OFF when a writer studies age-old techniques like alliteration. The ancient poets and lore masters of Greece, of the Nordic lands, of pre-Chaucerian England used alliteration as a way to make their stories memorable, and incidentally easier to memorize. Look at *Beowulf*, the *Canterbury Tales*, the *Iliad* or the *Odyssey*, and almost anything Shakespeare wrote, and see how effectively one can set the stage by echoing subtle sounds. It works even better if you read the selections out loud. Hamlet agonized over his choices with a fair number of S sounds; Juliet repeated her F's and E's as she expressed her terror at her proposed experiment with poison. All the B's in the third example may not make for great literature, but they certainly make the sentence memorable; and the hard K's and C's in the final example set a mood of wintry desolation.

Try it. Take anything you've written lately, and shift a few words here and there. Let your Inner Editor play a while with the sounds. See if you can say without saying, evoke a mood without spelling it out, ruminate in the moonlight, and tease a scene into telling a deeper story by using the sounds of the words as much as the meaning of the words themselves.

I dare you. The doing of it will double your delight. Oh dear!

Tips in Action

What did you always dream of doing?

If that dream is feasible, perhaps you could plan a way to make it work. If it's not feasible, you can still write it. Be willing to dream big. Be willing to follow a road you've avoided in the past. And, as long as you're writing for your own self-exploration, remember that you are not bound by any rules or regulations, nor are there any limits whatsoever on what you can do.

Stretch yourself, and see what happens. If it's illegal, be sure you keep it on paper only.

Dream big.
If that doesn't work, dream bigger.

39

Murdering Characters

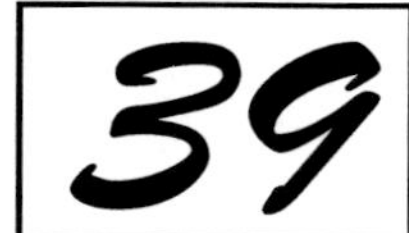

WHEN I CONFIDED to Brian Corrigan recently that I felt like I was floundering—my fifth murder mystery simply had not pulled together into any sort of cohesive story—he suggested that I kill off one of my favorite characters. If you've ever looked at Brian's website, www.brianjaycorrigan.com you'll know why he quickly added, "Don't hurt the cat, though!"

What happens when we murder a favorite character? Or, for that matter, when we make any kind of major shift in our way of doing things? Yes, a lot of fear comes up. Yes, some rebellion happens. Yes, we may feel disoriented for a good long time. As scary as change may be, however, we generally learn something positive from taking a new approach.

> *Yes, a lot of fear comes up.*

How can this process benefit a writer? Brian was right. Doing the unexpected not only makes for a more interesting plotline, it can jolt us out of complacency, that muddy swamp we too often find ourselves in as writers. If we take our characters for granted, we'll never let them grow. If we take our writing process for granted, we'll seldom find new dimensions that will surprise not only our readers, but ourselves as well.

Life coaching is an explosively evolving new field. Why has it taken hold now? I'd guess it is because so many of us have looked at our lives and seen lack rather than richness, have seen boredom rather than adventure, have seen the shallows rather than the ocean depths. For many of us, stepping from the old ways into something new is not easy, so we flock to life coaches to help guide us through to what we hope will be a brighter future.

A writer, even a very good writer, almost invariably benefits from a good writing coach, which is why I'm taking Brian's *Shape of Words* seminar for the second time. And out of it came his advice to kill somebody (a fictional character, that is!) that I was attached to. Talk about being jolted out of complacency. I've experienced rage, bewilderment, denial, and grief. I've cried about it, wailed over it, and sat for long stretches simply staring at nothing, wondering how I can ever do this and hold my head up at the book clubs I visit. And then, of course, I have laughed at the possibilities. That's what's fun about being a novelist. One can go to outrageous lengths; one can manipulate lives with no compunction whatsoever.

It's a heady feeling. If you're stuck in what you're writing, I strongly suggest that you kill off a character you love, observe your reactions, listen to your feelings, write it all down, and see what happens.

And if it doesn't work out, do a big fat rewrite.

Tips in Action

As it says in this essay, "Take chances with your protagonist. Put your main character up against a situation that scares him to the core of his being. Bring her to the point where she must face her deepest fear—and see the growth that occurs as a result. If he is basically honest, set up a scenario where that honesty could endanger a loved one. If she is driven by a need to control, rip that ability away from her and set her adrift."

Do it.

March of the Seasons

LAST MONTH MY favorite date came and went. The fourth of March, the only date in the year that gives writers a clear, concise, directive. *March forth!* it tells us every year. Some years I do, and some years I don't, but the advice is still clear. Find your own distinct voice and, with it playing the background music, march forward.

One hundred fifty-three years ago, Henry David Thoreau wrote that "if a man does not keep pace with his companions, perhaps it is because he hears a different drummer. Let him step to the music which he hears, however measured or far away." He coined a phrase that could well be the theme song for any writer who wants to pave a new route through the publishing world.

> *There are, after all, only thirty-five plots and perhaps four dozen archetypal characters available to us.*

Of course, we all know that there are no truly new ideas in writing, just as there are no new seasons. Try to tell that to your heart, though, when spring appears or when the first wilting day of summer comes. Surely there's never before been a spring so ethereal, nor a summer so bright. And there are, after all, only thirty-five plots and perhaps four dozen archetypal characters available to us. Yet, think of the variety that results when we imbue one of those characters in one of those plots with our own distinctive twist, our own particular whimsy. Or, for that matter, our own bizarre skullduggery.

The trick in learning to march forth to our own drummer is to study the craft of writing. Read the how-to books, take workshops. Don't just listen to speakers—take notes! Then, when we retire to write, the good advice we've heard or read will stick around. Above all, though, don't try to play it safe. Take chances with your protagonist. Put your main character up against a situation that scares him to the core of his being. Bring her to the point where she must face her deepest fear—and see the growth that occurs as a result. If he is basically honest, set up a scenario where that honesty could endanger a loved one. If she is driven by a need to control, rip that ability away from her and set her adrift. Remember, as long as you're writing, the work is in draft form. It may be draft number thirty-five, but it's still a work in progress until it's ready for publication.

If our characters do not grow, how can we as writers possibly enlarge our territory? I should think that only someone who is content with boredom will get sucked into formulaic writing. If you are a genre writer (mystery/suspense/romance/fantasy) there will be a certain amount of formula involved. Readers come to expect a thriller to be thrilling, a romance to be, well, romantic, and a fantasy to delve into other worlds unknown as yet to mere earthlings. Even with these expectations in mind, though, we can stretch our characters and our own writing ability by challenging the norm. Sit down at your keyboard and surprise yourself. March forth to that drummer you hear, and dance your way along your street, no matter what the season.

Tips in Action

List the light-bulb moments you've had over the past year or so. Or the past decade or so. Think about what those moments have meant to you in your growth as a writer.

If you think you haven't had any, shake yourself up a bit. Begin reading more, paying attention more. Take a class; learn a new skill. The light bulb's bound to go off somewhere in there.

Mother, May I?

MAY YOU? OF course you may, if you're a writer. That's the beauty of the writing life. We can take any character, any situation, any setting, and churn out a complete world. We can invent towns, people, crimes, romances, we can even change history to suit our needs, as long as we understand that first drafts (or second or third or twenty-fourth drafts) will eventually need to be honed to a marketable level.

How much can we invent? As much as we care to. As much as we're capable of inventing. How much can we get published, though? Ahh, to quote the master, "there's the rub."

> *"Maybe because that's how people talk?" In that light-bulb moment, he grew as a writer.*

I'm currently in the process of mentoring two very different young people, early teens both of them. The boy's book is a World War II action drama, filled with airplanes and people falling off cliffs, with guns and grenades. This morning we met at the library, and he told me he was reading Grisham's *The Firm*. "A lot of the paragraphs are just one sentence long," he said.

"And why do you think that is?"

He thought a moment. "Maybe because that's how people talk?"

In that light-bulb moment, he grew as a writer. His next draft, I dare say, will approach more closely that illusion of reality that we, as writers, try to impart. It's not just dialogue, although that, as you know, is vital in any novel. So we'll keep working on getting the conversations ironed out and, on top of that, we'll tackle the *sense of place*. I gave him an assignment. "After you finish *The Firm*," I said, "read *Airborn* by Ken Oppel, and watch not only the way Oppel handles dialogue, but the way he sets us firmly into the picture by evoking such vivid settings." I can't wait to see his cliff and his airplane hangar next time we meet.

The girl's book is an epic set on the frozen tundra, peopled (if you'll excuse that term) with reindeer and wolves, with bears and hawks. She and I met for a consultation last week. That library sees a lot of me.

"Do you think my character names are too confusing?" she asked.

That was easy. A one-word answer.

"But they all mean something," she objected, even though she was the one who had asked in the first place. "The reindeer language is quite complex."

"Yes, you've set it up that way," I told her. "Your average reader, though, is not going to care whether this name is a derivative of that name. If they're too much alike, you simply confuse your reader."

"But . . ."

But is the war cry of a writer who wants to justify a story line, a scene, some dialogue, a description, a name. *But* is very seldom valid. The reader who gets confused is never wrong. The reader is simply confused, most often because the writer was being obtuse, vague, esoteric, or negligent. If we hide a fact, we must put in a clue, a foreshadowing, an explanation. Otherwise, we're not being fair to our readers. If we invent a language or a country, we must make it workable in the minds of our readers.

So the question remains. Mother, may I?

Yes, you may. But your editor, with the well-being of your reader in mind, may make you change it.

Tips in Action

Read a book of jokes and have some good belly laughs. Laughing (at ourselves in particular) is quite a healthy practice.

Write your favorite funny experience. What did you learn from it?

Leaving Her Behind

ON THE WAY to the library this morning, I heard a reporter interviewing David Rabe, a playwright and novelist, who has been highly acclaimed by some critics and scorned by others.

At any rate, someone read from his latest novel, and one phrase jumped out at me:

> ". . . leaving her behind . . ."

I might as well have turned off the radio at that point, because I didn't hear another word of the interview. I saw a snarling dog leap at a fleeing shoplifter and rip out a satisfying pound of flesh. At which point the mangled woman ran offstage, (are you ready for this?) leaving her behind behind. Or some of it at least.

> *I saw a snarling dog leap at a fleeing shoplifter and rip out a satisfying pound of flesh.*

I know, I'm hopeless.

I am also patently sure that David Rabe never in his wildest dreams would have imagined that someone could be sidetracked by as simple a phrase as *leaving her behind.* It's all a matter of whether a word is a preposition (which is what he intended) or a noun (which is what I heard).

How can we possibly write in such a way that our readers will know clearly, absolutely, exactly what we mean? Well, the truth of the matter is that we can't. We simply do our best, and hope that the nutcase listening in the car on the way to the library won't run off the road while she guffaws about *leaving her behind . . . behind.*

Pathetic, isn't it?

Tips in Action

Buy a pack of 3 x 5 index cards. Invent a penpal, someone who will be enthusiastic about hearing from you.

Now start a correspondence. Make each "postcard" into
a chapter in the drama, rather like the "story" I told about
Archibald's fiancée in those two brief entries.

Have fun with it.

43

Precision Postcards

BROWSING THROUGH TREASURES at Coffee Buy the Book in Roswell, I came across Robert Olen Butler's *had a good time: stories from American postcards*. I've always been a sucker for a well-written postcard. Butler, according to the book jacket, collects early twentieth century picture postcards, and *had a good time* is a collection of short stories, each based on one of the cards. We even get photos of the cards—front and back.

There is an art to writing a postcard, one that we writers would do well to hone. My newest project—don't I need another one?—is to write postcard-length stories, as a number of writers have done before me. Reports from them suggest that this is harder to do than one might think. How does one get a beginning, a middle, and a satisfying end, into a square that measures three inches on a side?

> *I've always been a sucker for a well-written postcard.*

Write small.
Be concise.
Have fun.

Postcard #1
Tomorrow, I think. The second time the waiter spilled soup in Archibald's lap, I began to think he—Archibald, not the waiter—must have already been suspicious, since I was so careful not to betray anything in my countenance—nothing, that is, except concern for his dear sweet self. And the bouillabaisse stains on his pinstripes. A miniscule drop splashed on the hem of my yellow silk, but I didn't mention that to the waiter, who was positively abject with apologies. I plan to wear the yellow to his funeral—Archibald's, not the waiter's— before I leave for Paris. See you <u>soon</u>, my dearest.

Postcard #2
Well, mum, she tried it again. You were right, as usual. So sorry I ignored your advice. Not that I'm particularly worried about the outcome. So transparent. Why didn't I see it as clearly as you did? Had to trip the blundering fool twice. If she could pay him, I can pay him more. Tonight, I think. Then I'll be home for a good long rest. After the funeral.

Tips in Action

Write your vision statement. What is your purpose in life?

Dig deep. Your resources may surprise you.

44

Vision - Who Are You?

DID YOU EVER wonder who writes those author bios on the book jackets? Did you ever wish you knew more about a particular writer? If you, like I, have been disappointed sometimes in the sparse information—*Shelly Writer lives with her husband and two dogs in northern Oklahoma*—you might look on Shelly Writer's website. There you are likely to find a button that says *About Me* or *FAQs*. So go ahead and read all about Shelly.

Then plan what you'll say on your own website. I've been working with a business coach. Yes—writing is a business. He didn't like my *About Me* button. He suggested that I write a vision statement in the form of what he called a corporate culture position paper. Sounds a bit intimidating, doesn't it? And why on earth would something like that be necessary for writers when all we want to do is write?

> *I am 100% responsible for my thoughts, my actions, and my responses at all times.*

This turned out to be one of the most worthwhile tasks I've approached lately, and I thoroughly recommend it to you. I chose to take my name—I know, you don't have to say it; it's a schoolgirl approach—and turn the first letters into my statement. When you read this, you will know who I am, much more than anything that says *Fran Stewart lives with various rescued cats by a creek on the backside of Hog Mountain, Georgia.*

Because of space restraints, I can't put the whole statement here. For now, let's look only at the letters that spell FRAN:

Far-seeing: I have developed a sense of perspective in my life, and I understand that while all things change, always, there is a more basic way in which we are all one; we are all connected; we are all the same.

Responsible: Since I believe that thought is creative, I am 100% responsible for my thoughts, my actions, and my responses at all times. I am someone who lights a candle to dispel darkness. If I find darkness around me, I know it is time to light another candle.

Accountable: What I promise to do, I do to the best of my ability, using all the resources at my disposal.

Nurturing: I choose to be kind, to encourage others, to lend a helping hand when one is wanted. In all circumstances, I speak well of people. In all my actions, I look for the highest good that I can offer, and I act from compassion, knowing that other people do not need me to *fix* them, as they are not *broken*.

In my work as a writer, an editor, a speaker, I hold to these principles. If you ask me to meet with your writers group or your book club, or if you want me to speak to your organization or teach a writing seminar, this is what you will get. Naturally, I'd like you to visit my website www.franstewart.com and check out the rest of my name as well. And then email me with *your* culture statement. Who are you? What do you believe in? What does your writing reflect?

If you haven't thought about it, chances are good that all we'll ever know about you is that you live with a spouse and two dogs in northern Oklahoma.

Tips in Action

Pick a book you enjoy. Talk to a friend about it.

What? You don't have a friend you can talk to about books? Find some new friends.

Meanwhile, write what you think about the book and why you think it.

45

Book Clubs – the Last Bastion of Literacy?

THE LAST TIME I was interviewed on the radio, this was one of the questions:

"According to a report of the Independent Book Publishing Association, over five million American adults belong to reading groups. Why do Americans love books so much?"

That sounds like an encouraging statistic, doesn't it? Luckily, I knew about the question ahead of time, so I could formulate an answer, or at least the idea of an answer. Even without an interviewer asking, this is something that we as writers should think about. Without readers, we would be nowhere.

> *I threw out my TV set fourteen years ago.*

This country was founded by people who believed that unless people could read, they couldn't vote intelligently. That still holds true today. The thought of five million Americans reading and discussing books is quite positive. I've seen statistics, though, that say that 30% of American adults are to some extent illiterate. That is not only shocking but disturbing as well. When people vote based on sound bites put together by marketing companies, or speech writers' blurbs, then we ultimately get the government we deserve.

It's good that there are five million people in book clubs. And there are many other people who love books but don't join a reading group. That still leaves a couple of hundred million people who depend on television for their information and entertainment. I encourage people to buy books, particularly through independent bookstores, since that is one way to ensure that freedom of information will continue in this country.

I'm going to keep buying books by writers whose work I enjoy. That's the way to be sure that quality books will always be available. I also threw out my TV set fourteen years ago. Try it, and then, if your heart leads you in that direction, perhaps you could consider volunteering with an adult literacy group.

Go on. I dare you. It's a good idea.

Give me a good book any day.

Tips in Action

- Your favorite teacher was _______________________________________.

- This teacher opened your mind to the _______________________________

  ____

  ____

  ____.

- You have passed on that legacy by doing what? _____________________

  ____

  ____

  ____.

46

The Legacy of Teachers

A YEAR AGO, in October of 2006, I started my keynote address to the Georgia Council of Teachers of English by singing "Heaven, I'm in heaven . . ." I've never been intimidated about speaking to large groups, even though for most people, fear of public speaking is even greater than their fear of dying. And those 350 teachers? I loved it. My speech at the GCTE's annual convention was a recounting of the three English teachers who changed my life. Without those three blessed people, I would not be the person I am, the writer I am, today. They led me into a wonder world of books, and they insisted that I take responsibility for my actions; they encouraged me, and they made me hone my writing skills, because they would not accept anything less than my best effort.

> *For most people, fear of public speaking is even greater than their fear of dying.*

Last month, on a book tour in Colorado, I was invited to speak to a much smaller, but equally important, group of teachers—the middle school and high school teachers in the small town of Florence. Listening to their comments afterwards, about how much they appreciated hearing someone acknowledge the gift that teachers give on a daily basis, made me very glad that I'd taken the time years ago to write thank-you notes to the teachers who had influenced me. The thank-you notes I received in return made it worthwhile. Now that I'm old enough that most of my teachers have left this earth, I'm doubly glad I took the time.

I'd like to encourage you to sit down right now and pen a note to a teacher who made a positive difference in your life. You see, if it weren't for that teacher, you might never have discovered the breadth and depth of rich experience that a world of reading could bring to you. If it weren't for that teacher, you might not be a writer today.

Do it now, before it's too late.

Tips in Action

List ten kinds of silence you've encountered over the past month.

- ____________________
- ____________________
- ____________________
- ____________________
- ____________________
- ____________________
- ____________________
- ____________________
- ____________________
- ____________________

What responses did each type elicit from you?

How can you use these experiences in your writing?

47

The Many Kinds of Silence

AFTER THE FUROR of the holidays, we tend to long for silence in a world where silence seems not to be readily available. This month my challenge to you is to explore, investigate, list, appreciate the many kinds of silence.

We are, after all, writers. This assignment—and whether or not you choose to accept it, this tape will *not* self-destruct—is, on the surface, simple. It's rather elegant, in fact. Simply listen. Listen to what you do hear. Then listen to what you do not hear. Compare the two.

> *Listen to what you do hear. Then listen to what you do not hear. Compare the two.*

I think it would be safe to say that most people associate silence with nighttime. Fifty years ago, in October of 1957, when I was in fifth grade, my father bundled me up in a gray and black blanket late one night and took me outside to watch the sky over Colorado Springs. Sputnik, the first human-made orbiting intrusion into space, tumbled its way across the background of stars. (In 1957 one could still see jillions of stars.) Against their spangles, Sputnik skipped in eerie silence. Eerie because I was old enough to have picked up on my parents' fears about the possible launch of ballistic missiles.

In school, over the next number of months, we had drills in which we sat—in silence, another kind of silence—beneath our desks with our heads ducked beneath our arms for protection. That was a silence stippled with fear and later, when the drills became old hat, and when we realized the enormity of what a nuclear attack would entail, with desks as scant protection, those were silences laced with derision.

We all have had numerous instances of silence in our lives. The silence of sitting next to a sick child, listening to each labored breath. The silence of that moment when we know the fever has turned and all will be well. The silence of sitting with a dying parent, knowing that the next breath might be the last. The silence of hearing that last breath and waiting for another that will never come. The silence of walking through a woodland park, unaware of the thunder from the interstate just one mile away, listening to the multi-faceted silence of birdsong, coupled with the awareness that that particular kind of silence used to be a lot louder before pesticides and fertilizers and clear-cutting destroyed so many of our songbirds.

There are three separate kinds of silence of thinking—or agonizing—in a high school class
before, during, and after an exam. There were the unique yet universally constant kinds of
silence when each of those students swam in the womb before birth, silence attended by
the constant, and therefore seemingly unremarkable, swish of the mother's breathing and
the pounding of her heartbeat, a silence we cannot consciously recall because it came to us
before we had language—language!—with which to define it. There is the silence now when
we may sit with quiet around us, yet feel bombarded by questions and concerns from within
that we cannot silence.

There is the lyrical silence of a butterfly composing a light show on a summer afternoon.
There is the frantic silence of a cockroach, disturbed in a kitchen drawer, scurrying to dive
beneath a soup ladle.

There is the silence of writing, delving deep within ourselves to find the apt word, the cogent
turn of phrase, the sentence that will bring cohesion to our often jumbled thoughts.

There is the silence now of ending this essay—my writing it, your reading it—and the
increased awareness of the impact of silence. Pull out your ever-present notebook. You are
a writer; of course you have a notebook at hand! Begin to list the silences you remember
and the ones you forgot to remember. List the silences around you now. List the silences you
hear—or don't hear—in your car, in your front yard, in your backyard, in the elevator. Notice
the sounds that are so much a part of the background of your life, that your brain has shifted
them into a realm of unhearing, of unawareness. The sounds that you don't hear say so much
about you as a person and, most definitely, as a writer.

Tips in Action

- Head to the library.

- Look in the children's or young adult's section.

- Check out a book.

- Read it.

- Write something about your response to it.

Children's Books

VOLUNTEERING IN MY granddaughter's elementary school library has turned out to be one of the best time commitments I ever made as a writer. It's hard not to check out books every week—in fact, I don't even try to resist—and I've found a wealth of writing instruction there before me.

Perhaps you're like me; you write for adults. Why read books written for children? Well, for one thing, they're pretty darn good. I've been concentrating on the Newberry Award lists, and I've found some treasures. It's not just the gripping story lines, either. I've been reminded with each book how important it is for a writer, regardless of the age level of the reader, to breathe life into the scenery, to flesh out the people, to avoid the easy ending. In other words, to write effectively.

I'm going to point you toward only three of the many authors I've come to love over my past two years as a library volunteer.

If you have never met Margaret Peterson Haddix and her *Shadow Children* series, start with *Among the Hidden* and read them all for a thoroughly chilling and completely edifying account of how a few individuals can make a difference when they act with courage in the face of seemingly all-pervasive evils.

Read them all for a thoroughly chilling and completely edifying account of how a few individuals can make a difference when they act with courage in the face of seemingly all-pervasive evils.

Mary Downing Hahn's *Daphne's Book* came highly recommended by the school librarian. If you ever felt as a child that you were always on the outside looking in, Hahn's story will undoubtedly resonate with your soul as it did with mine. This tale teaches us as writers to trust when our well-defined characters lead us into unexpected byways.

Finally, Gail Carson Levine enchanted me with her *Ella Enchanted*. How I wish this timeless story, published in 1998, had been available when my children were young. It's comforting to see that all these books have long lists of return dates stamped on the backs. Children are reading them and, hopefully, are absorbing those basic tenets of fine writing—fabulous

characters driving superb plots through believable countryside, all the while speaking the way people speak. What better use for the English language?

I'd encourage you to head for the children's section of your local library and absorb these examples of writing at its best. When you find some favorite authors of your own, please send word. I'm at fran@franstewart.com, and I'd love to hear from you.

Tips in Action

Write a straightforward set of dialogue with at least five lines of speech.

Now, using the examples I've given you, rewrite your dialogue four or five ways, varying the characters, the relationships between those characters, the mood, and/or the level of intensity.

Which ones work best? Have you used attribution effectively? What could you change to make each little snippet more compelling?

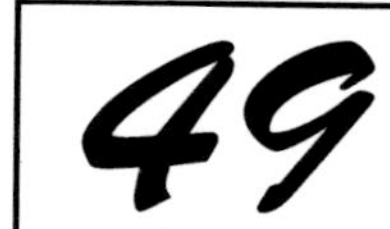

He Said/She Said:
The Ups and Downs of Dialogue

ATTRIBUTION IS THE fancy word that refers to the ways in which we make clear just who is saying what in our stories. We can, however, go far beyond the tried and true *he said/she said.* Those attributions work almost invisibly because people read right across them. If you reverse your attribution to *said he/said she*, you're running a bit of a risk, because those words are more likely to be noticed, to get in the way of what you're trying to indicate.

The trick is to use just enough attribution to keep the reader from becoming confused. If you have two women conversing, for instance, an occasional *Martha said* or *Sarah said* will certainly serve to keep us straight. In the long run, though, too many of those will get boring. The reason is that people never *simply* talk. They shift around, they sit, or they stand. They glower; they simper. They scratch their noses or their ears. They pull little pills off their sweaters.

> *People never simply talk. They shift around, they sit, or they stand. They glower; they simper. They scratch their noses or their ears. They pull little pills off their sweaters.*

Try watching people as they converse. How many times do they make eye contact? How many times do they avoid it? What can you infer about their relationship just from watching them talk or not talk to each other? How do they move? What do they *do?*

Naturally, there will be gender differences. Women tend to make more eye contact in a friendly conversation and less in a confrontational one. With men it's the opposite. These last two sentences are sweeping generalizations, I admit, but they are ones you can use as a writer to enliven the dialogue in your stories.

Here's a fairly straightforward piece of dialogue that is easy to follow, but hardly illuminating as far as the character of each speaker is concerned. Because it is a question and answer session, we can clearly tell who's saying what without any attribution whatsoever.

    "Did you take out the garbage yet?"
    "No."
    "Why not?"

"I didn't want to."
"When will you do it?"
"In the morning."

Now let's turn it into a story through attributions.

Mama didn't even look at me. "Did you take out the garbage yet?"
"No." I tried not to whine, but my voice came out higher than I wanted it to. When she slammed the dish towel down on the counter, I knew I was in trouble.
"Why not?" she yelled.
I ducked behind the table. "I didn't want to."
There was a long silence. "When . . . will . . . you . . . do it?"
I couldn't face the storm outside. I just couldn't. It scared the dickens out of me. She should have known that. "In the morning," I promised, but she still wasn't happy.

Or how about this one:

"Did you take out the garbage yet?"
"No," Paul said.
George drummed his fingers on the tablecloth. "Why not?"
Paul took his time answering. "I didn't want to." He moved his salad fork half an inch to one side.
"When," George asked, "will you do it?"
"In the morning." Paul lifted his wine glass, smirked, and took the tiniest sip.

Each of these dialogues gives us a feel for who the people are and what their relationship is to each other. Showing action gives the attribution *and* furthers the story line at the same time.

If you have three or more people talking at once, you'd better be pretty sure that they all have distinctive speech characteristics that will differentiate them from each other. One person might use slang; another could be the kind who never finishes a sentence. One could be formal; another could constantly speak in questions.

Pete slapped his fist into his left palm. "Didja take out the garbage yet?"
"No . . . no, I . . ."
"Why not?" Ralph interrupted.
"I . . . I didn't want to."
"When ya gonna do it?"
"In the . . . in the morning?"
Pete looked at Ralph and shook his head. Bunco didn't stand a chance.

If their speech patterns are not that easy to tell apart, then your attributions have to be even more concise:

> "Did you take out the garbage yet?" Marla asked her son.
> "No," Bobby said.
> Sheila looked at her brother-in-law in disgust. "Why not?"
> "I didn't want to." He yawned and didn't bother to cover his mouth.
> Sheila grimaced as Marla sighed. "When will you do it?"
> Bobby turned his back on Sheila and grinned at his mother. "In the morning," he said.

Attributions should always propel the story forward. If you listen, really listen, to how people speak, and if you watch them, *really watch them*, while they're speaking, you should be able to pick up quite a few tips on how to make your written dialogue more interesting and more useful. Notebooks ready? Listen. Watch. Write.

Tips in Action

We're writers, so sharing our written word is important to us. Think about visiting a book club. They'll want you to read a brief section from your book. That's where the written word sometimes conflicts with the spoken word.

- Choose a chapter from the book you're working on now.

- Stand in front of a big mirror.

- Read the entire chapter aloud.

- Underline what you stumble over. If it doesn't speak well, why ever would you want to include it?

- Rewrite the awkward parts.

- Read it again.

- Whew! Doesn't that feel better?

50

A New Language

I WOKE ONE Sunday morning to a discussion between Krista Tippett and a woman who is an expert on the writings of Rumi, the 13th century Persian poet and mystic. My Sunday radio alarm is set to 7 a.m., when WABE (90.1 FM) presents *Speaking of Faith*, a National Public Radio program. Although I always keep a notebook beside my bed—what true writer is ever without a notebook handy?—still, I'm not always alert enough at that hour of the morning to get quotations precisely right. The gist of the Rumi line that she quoted, though, was this: "Learn a new language so you can see a new world."

> *"Learn a new language so you can see a new world."*

Learn a new language is good advice indeed, particularly for ethnocentric Americans who believe that English ought to be good enough for everyone. Despite the fact that English has gradually been adopted as an international language for politics and commerce, the very nature of a language reflects the mindset of its speakers. The ways in which American English is evolving is a reflection of the new dynamics that rule American culture. *Eddress*, for instance. This shortened form of *e-mail address* has the advantage of being concise and logical. I'd call that a good evolution.

I met the president of my Alma Mater recently at a gathering for Illinois Wesleyan University alumni in the Atlanta area. Dick Wilson believes that people who graduate from IWU should be able to write well. How earthshaking is this? Could you meet his challenge? Probably you could, if you are a member of the Atlanta Writers Club. How many of the excellent ideas generated in the business world, though, lie unused for want of someone to write them out clearly, logically?

One of the alumni at the gathering said, "Give me an accountant who can write an intelligible paragraph, and I'll show you someone who will own the company soon." How sad that connecting one coherent sentence to another and yet another is a skill beyond the reach of some—should I say *many?*—college graduates. It is deplorable that the vocabulary of most TV programs and magazine articles is kept to a fourth-grade level. I find it hard to believe that many people are unwilling to attend a performance of Shakespeare because of a fear that the language will be too difficult to understand. Still, those plays were written for ordinary

people, many of whom were illiterate in terms of written language, but who had a depth of knowledge about the spoken word that far surpasses anything we're exposed to today.

So, as we are impelled by Rumi's advice to "learn a new language," we may find that the language we have to learn first is our own. As we explore the surprising depth of the English language, we will discover new vistas opening before us, allowing us truly to see a new world. After that? Let's go on to learn Spanish, French, and a little Greek, eh?

Tips in Action

Here's the assignment: Buy a book today. If you want book-stores to stay in business, find a small bookstore and buy your book there. It is not enough to walk in and say, "Oh, I just love your store." Show that love at the cash register.

When bookstores abound, you as a writer will have more options for getting the word out about *your* book.

- Read the book you just bought.

- Share your enthusiasm for it with a friend.

- Buy another copy (at that same bookstore) to give as a gift.

51

The First Agreement - Impeccability

"BE IMPECCABLE IN your word." This is the first of *The Four Agreements* discussed by Manuel Ruiz in his book by that title. Despite how imaginative our writing is—I, after all, write murder mysteries with a cat who makes comments in italics throughout the books—we still have a responsibility as writers to present a world that is true to its own internal logic. Albert Einstein remarked once that "Knowledge is limited; . . . imagination encircles the world." The world of imagination that fiction writers inhabit is as varied as the range of writers themselves, yet within that broad scope, fiction writers must present a world that makes some sort of ultimate sense to the reader.

> *My word is my reputation.*

Lewis Carroll's *Alice's Adventures in Wonderland* is a classic in the mixed-up genre of truly imaginative fiction, yet one can follow an absurd sense of logic throughout all of Alice's rambles, as each zany character, from the pontificating caterpillar to the grinning Cheshire Cat, gives Alice a clue about how to function in her own world. The point is, we're willing to follow her from the time she goes down the rabbit hole until she's safely out of it at the end, because Carroll has impeccably adhered to his own sense of *logic*, such as it is.

There are writers who tie up every loose end in a novel. There are those of us who see the ongoing series as the unit of expression, who are willing to leave a few unanswered questions, teasers if you will, from one book to the next. I'm reminded of Sue Grafton, who got all the way to O in her alphabetical mystery series before she revealed anything at all about Kinsey Milhone's first ex-husband. That's fourteen earlier books that say zip, nada, nottink about him, yet, because of the internal logic of the series and the believability of the protagonist, we are willing to accept the long wait, and say *eureka* when we finally find out what had been going on all those years ago in Milhone's life.

Impeccability has to do with more than just the story line, though. It revolves around the craft of the writing itself. Who are we to stand up and ask people to put down good money for our books if our books are less than our best effort? For this very reason, I have a tendency to check out a book by an unfamiliar author from the library first. If I like the writing, if I'm caught up by the story, if the words themselves are well-thought-out and well-put-together, then and only then do I buy the book. As an author myself, how well I know the importance of book sales—how else could I buy all that cat food for my hungry felines? I choose to encourage good writing by buying good books. It's as simple as that. Because I ask people to buy my books, I choose to be impeccable about buying the books of other good writers, as well as impeccable about the way I craft my stories. My word is my reputation. My words are my reputation. I choose impeccability.

Tips in Action

Take that novel you're working on and see how it charts.

- Draw a symbol for your protagonist at the center of a big blank page.

- Place the other characters—the main ones—in a circle around her, varying the distances from her based on how strong you perceive their connection to be.

- Now draw lines from her to them. Some lines will be heavy supporting strands, some may simply be dots, some may end up being arrows going one way or both ways.

- Next, plot the connections among those secondary characters.

- Be sure you've put your antagonist in there somewhere.

- See if your web will support itself.

  - Is it anchored by setting?

  - Is it set astir by the breezes of effective dialogue?

  - Will it weather the storm of intrigue you've written in there?

- Enjoy the process.

Spiders and Ants

ARACHNOPHOBIA IS NOT a problem of mine. I like spiders. I like ants, also. Did you ever think about the common ground that spiders and ants share in the animal kingdom? They both go to uncommon lengths to achieve results that often—due to wind, rain, someone's head, a hiker's boots—are destroyed before a tasty bug is caught in the web or before the baby ants hatch from their white rice-shaped larval bodies.

Now what does this have to do with the craft of writing? Oh come now, we meet deadlines as industriously as many an ant. We spin our spider webs of words with diligence. For those of us who are self-employed, our next meal may very well depend on that spinning. People who've made the study of spiders their life work tell me that baby spiders have to learn the art of web-spinning. They may know instinctively how to extrude their silken web material, just as humans seem to have a built-in drive to use language, but turning that initial instinct into a shining web is the learning of a lifetime.

> *We spin our spider webs of words with diligence. For those of us who are self-employed, our next meal may very well depend on that spinning.*

One humid morning a number of years ago, I walked outside at dawn and saw the *spirea* bushes covered in a white haze of miniscule spider webs. Each web spanned only the inch or so between arching branches of the full shrub. The spiders were too tiny for my eyes, although I could detect a tiny swelling in the center of each web. I can only assume that the spider was there, waiting for prey that lived at some microscopic scale. Each single web was almost too small for notice, but the thousands of them that connected the *spirea* sprays sparkled as the rising sun caught the moisture that coated each strand of web. Dew is too solid a word for that form of water. It was almost as though Mother Earth thought "damp," and the wetness appeared. As much as I have looked for it, I never again saw that magical combination of just the right humidity, just the right slant of sun, and just that plenitude of tiny webs.

I feel a similar astonishment when I read a truly magical book, one in which the characters walk off the page and into my heart. The writer spins an exact blend of plot elements with

beauty of structure, absence of "formula," and expert weaving of words to capture the tasty bug of my imagination. I wonder if baby spiders watch their elders at work and learn from them how to craft their webs, just as I read books by established authors, take writing workshops, and listen to my wonderful editor. Noting my tendency to overuse passive verbs in the most recent draft of my fifth mystery, Nanette Littlestone—editor extraordinaire— recently wrote, ". . . with so many words in the English language, Fran, you could avail yourself of the many possibilities." *Ouch!* My inner baby spider started to work on my next web/draft much chagrined and much inspired.

During the rewriting process, I often trudge, like a single ant in a long line. I cart one simile or metaphor at a time to the anthill of my novel, feeding the narrative, tending the people who live in my brain 24/7/365 (or 366 this particular year). I am both the ant and the anthill. I am the leaf segment and the cricket wing. I am predator, prey, and vegetation alike. Like the ant, I defend my boundaries, respect those of other ants, carry my part of the load, and share my bits of leaf with family, friends, and colleagues. Ants as a group are mostly beneficial to humans. Their tunneling mixes and aerates the soil. Writers are, or of right ought to be, beneficial as well. We tunnel through mounds of information and create fertile soil from a mixture of air, sand, water, words, and magic.

We writers spill the silk of our lifeblood onto the very pages of our books. We dig deep within ourselves to people our stories, our poems. We spin or trudge every day. We pay attention to the world we experience, and we extrude those sights and sounds, smells, tastes, and textures into webs that inform or entrance. Writers do not only entertain, they inspire; they move mountains.

What leaf will you carry? What will you spin today?

Tips in Action

What is the purpose of your writing? Think of five or six reasons why you write. Prioritize them, and list them here:

1. ____

2. ____

3. ____

4. ____

5. ____

6. ____

Instead of trying to prop up the sixth (least important) one on that list, concentrate on the first. What can you do today, what can you learn, that will help you promote that first reason?

- If you need to take a class, sign up for it now.

- If you need to write, sit down and do it.

- If you need to send a query, write it and send it.

53

Aristotle's Final Cause

DESPITE ALL THE hype about internet research—*Fast! Efficient! Extensive!*—give me a good old hard cover encyclopedia as a source for new ideas any day. Recently I paged through my *New Illustrated Columbia Encyclopedia*, copyright 1979, and found that Aristotle "posited four causes or principles of explanation: the **material** cause (the substance of which the thing is made); the **formal** cause (its design); the **efficient** cause (its maker or builder); and the **final** cause (its purpose or function). In modern thought," the article went on to say, "the efficient cause is generally considered the central explanation of a thing, but for Aristotle the final cause had primacy."

Hmmm. Food for thought. I spend a great deal of time in these *Tip of My Pen* columns extolling the virtues of the writing life, advising the use of good technical skills in writing, and praising the inner writer in each of us. I've taken on a large percentage of my duty as a writer to encourage other writers (Aristotle's efficient causes) to create polished works of art. I've lauded the writing impulse, whether the end result is a published novel, a collection of poetry, or a daily and very private journal. In other words, I've inadvertently focused on promoting the "efficient cause," the writer.

> *Without its function, the Declaration of Independence would be just another historical, difficult-to-decipher document.*

Perhaps I've missed the boat. Maybe Aristotle was right. The function of any piece of writing would be what? To inform? To educate? To entertain? To persuade? Without its function, the Declaration of Independence would be just another historical, difficult-to-decipher document. Without its purpose, Marianne Williamson's "Our Deepest Fear" poetic essay would be a string of beautifully-stated words, advertising Ms. Williamson herself. When we look at the function of those two documents, though, and the purpose behind them, we see that both writings changed the world.

I've long been a fan of the mystery genre. When I set out to write mysteries, though, I saw my purpose go far beyond the entertaining yarn. In each book, I deal with social issues and concerns—environmental responsibility, suicide prevention, the long-term effects of childhood sexual abuse, organic gardening. Perhaps my need to leave a legacy of knowledge

(rather than simply a legacy of words, no matter how well-crafted) has been my unconscious way of buying into Aristotle's premise.

If you can walk into the largest library you can find, look around at all the volumes there, and honestly say, "I have something to add to this heritage," then I'd say to you, "Go for it!" Let's both of us, though, step away from the admittedly riveting desire to see our names on title pages and ask what the final cause for our writing is. If we write to make the world a better place, Aristotle will, I am sure, nod his agreement.

Tips in Action

Step aside from that manuscript you're stuck on. Go ahead; write a crummy first draft of something else altogether—at least three full pages.

Give yourself permission simply to write. You can sift later.

Did you go someplace in this draft that was unexpected? Is there a nugget in there that you can use on the project you set aside?

54

Colanders or Plastic Cups –
The Fine Art of Sifting Words

PUT FIFTY OR sixty small stones in a wide sand box. Add two children and a variety of old kitchen utensils. Hand each child a bucket to fill, and watch what happens. One will scoop up handfuls or cupfuls of sand. The other will take the old dented colander and nestle it over the bucket, then pour the sand through, sorting out the stones in the very process of filling the container. Which kind of writer are you?

I find that when I begin a novel, I often scoop handfuls of words onto the page, filling it in a frenzy, anxious not to misplace an idea, an inspiration. I mix my metaphors, scatter too many words like *little* and *very*, and pepper my page with a multitude of adverbs, like a pizza with too many boring mushrooms and not enough spicy pepperoni.

> **All that searching allows me to see the holes, and see the possibilities, too.**

I wish I were more the colander sort. That would save me countless hours of rewriting before I got around to the *real* revisions. Why on earth do I condemn myself to searching for *little* and *very* when it would make more sense to sift them out at the start? Then I could pay attention to scene setting and sensory cues, landscape and character drawing, dialogue and drama building, all those truly important aspects of developing a novel that sings.

But the truth is I'm not a colander. I'm a scooper. And that's okay. By the time I've spilled my guts onto the page, I'm ready for some judicious cleaning up. Looking for *little* and *very* and all those mushrooms forces me to consider alternatives. I've been known to delete entire paragraphs. Heck, I've cut out whole chapters that didn't work. All that searching allows me to see the holes, and see the possibilities, too. Where can I take out stones? How can I add crystals instead? Should I delete this mushroom? Where's the pepperoni?

Ahh! The crummy first draft. What would we ever do without it?

Tips in Action

What do you want to be? This is the time to dream. Write it down here—what you really want.

Look at what you've written. See if an idea grows wings.

55

Whaddya Wanna Be?

I RECENTLY PICKED up the newspaper and found an article about a sixteen-year-old who was heading off to the State House to do a stint as a legislative page. The article quoted him as saying that he's always been interested in politics, ever since he ran for class president in fourth grade. He won that election. In Ronald Reagan's inaugural address, if I remember correctly, he mentioned having run for school offices as well. He lost them.

Now, I don't know about you, but when I entered fourth grade, politics wasn't an issue. I'd already read *Little Women* a dozen or so times. "Are you checking this out again, Frances?" The Air Force base librarian peered at me over the edge of the checkout desk and asked the same question every time I went in there. "Yes, ma'am," I assured her. She positively glowed when I finally discovered the *Black Stallion* series. "We have a lot of these books," she told me. Then I went on to read each of them at least six times, much to her dismay. For the rest of fourth grade, all I wanted to do was write stories and re-read every book ever written by Walter Farley.

> *If you want to be a politician, start off by running for office in grade school. If you want to be anything else of value, read.*

Blessed by a mother who never saved anything except her own salt and pepper collection as we moved from air base to air base, the library was a constant in my life. Who needed to own books when I had shelf after shelf available to me? The point is, fourth grade politicians turn into political adults, I guess. And fourth grade readers turn into, well, into anything they want to.

I admit a bias against people who can't find time to read a book. The most interesting people I meet generally get around to saying, "I always loved reading."

What does this mean? If you want to be a politician, start by running for office in grade school. If you want to be anything else of value, read. What a novel idea if all our politicians were well-read. Maybe they could start with the Constitution?

Tips in Action

Start with these five smells, then list five more.

Try to find a word or phrase to approximate each of them.

Are you satisfied with the results? If not, keep looking.

- fish ____

- burning paper _______________________________________

- sweat ____

- mountain air ____

- the shore at low tide _________________________________

- ____

- ____

- ____

- ____

- ____

56

Skunks and Stinky Feet

OKAY, SO MAYBE I should have put roses in the title, but really, don't you think those are a bit overworked in the odor category? Smell is one of the least-addressed senses in our lexicon. English—and if you've been reading this column with any sort of regularity, you *know* how much I love this language—simply falls short when it comes to smelly stuff.

Think about it. What word is there to describe fresh doughnuts? How would you sum up the scent of your own blood when you cut your finger? Did you ever think about the smell of a new car? Plenty of money goes into making sure that new cars (and some used ones, as well) smell new, and we all know what that scent *is*—can't you call it to mind right now?—but how would you *describe* it?

When faced with the dearth of words that epitomize *smell,* we generally resort to simile or metaphor. This works, as long as we don't overdo it. Plowing through a sea of similes is like swimming in a school of goldfish—the tickling

> *Someone who lifts the sheets out of the dryer and buries her nose in them is probably a happy character.*

gets to you after a while. So, here's your challenge, if you choose to accept it. Describe the following smells using a simile or a metaphor for each one. Then try it without a single simile or metaphor. See? We don't have words for smells, other than the usual tired ones, such as *fresh* or *pungent* or *aromatic* (whatever that means).

Newly cut grass, stinky feet on a sweaty four-year-old, the first fish you ever caught. What about a soft old queen-sized sheet straight out of the dryer, your own forearm (go ahead— smell it!), furniture polish, or that herbal pain relief rub you used this morning. Have you ever smelled three-day-old roadkill, or fresh horse manure? Use words to paint the air just before a rainstorm and the air right after a rainstorm.

On the other hand, why do we have to describe the smells? Go back over that list. With the possible exception of the feet and the roadkill, you probably already know what each item smells like. Your readers will, too. Someone who lifts the sheets out of the dryer and buries her nose in them is probably a happy character. Someone who pulls out the sheets, collapses

into a heap and buries her nose in them is most likely in need of comfort, a need that most of us can identify with.

Explore the world of smells. Use them to pepper your writing (sparsely). A tasty dish indeed.

Tips in Action

If you were a punctuation mark, which one would you be and why?

- asterisk *
- brackets [ ]
- caret ^
- colon :
- comma ,
- exclamation point !
- hyphen -
- long dash —
- parentheses ( )
- period .
- question mark ?
- quotes " "
- semi-colon :
- slash /
- underline ___

57

Punc!tu?a-tion:
Invisible Ally or Obnoxious Intruder?

YESTERDAY I SPOKE with a friend who sneezed halfway through our conversation. It sounded like an exclamation point, emphasizing the somewhat acerbic comment she'd just made.

This morning I had a different sort of conversation with another woman, someone who is always timid about where she stands, ready to acquiesce to any forcefully-stated opinion. Each sentence of hers holds an underlying question mark, as if she needs permission for every word she utters.

I've read authors who seemed to be in love with certain punctuation marks, some of which were more obtrusive than others. I'm sure we've all been told: "No more than one exclamation point per chapter," or per *book* if we have particularly exacting editors. There are times, however, when excessive punctuation can help to delineate a character. I've written a minor figure in my mystery series whose unremitting enthusiasm grates on the nerves of her tap dance students. Naturally I write her with exclamation points, sometimes four to a speech.

> *The trick is to make punctuation relatively invisible so it never intrudes on your reader's attention to the story.*

That is dialogue, though, and her exclamation points form a specific device to lend credence to that specific character's persona. I limit—strictly—the number of times she speaks in any given scene because after a while, such bouncy energy is as exhausting to the reader as a puppy who won't settle down is to a cat lover.

The long dash, called an em dash in the printing industry, is another often overworked piece of punctuation. Semicolons seem to have fallen into disfavor these days, supplanted by that upstart em, possibly because it's easier to scratch (or type) a long dash than it is to decide between a colon and a semicolon. Or should that be a comma?

Ah! (there's my one exclamation point; did you notice it?) the ubiquitous comma, with so many rules governing its use, that it marches through series of words, separating them, blending them, and hopefully lending a semblance of order and clear meaning, as anyone

who has read the title *Eats Shoots and Leaves* can attest. Some writers are comma-happy, slapping them in place, sprinkling them around, and generally leaving behind a sense of pleasant chaos. Who, after all, other than an editor, can object to an extra comma or two? Multiple unnecessary commas, though, may leave us feeling as if a preoccupied housecleaner had shaken out the dust bag over a newly vacuumed carpet. Comma-happy authors tend to reason that it is better to have too many commas than none at all. I would vote for clarity, though, and the use of commas only to lend pauses and breathing spaces (and meaning) to an otherwise jumbled patois of words.

I'd suggest that you glance through your own writing now to see how you use punctuation. Count your exclamation points and your em dashes, your parentheses and your question marks. The trick is to make punctuation relatively invisible so it never intrudes on your reader's attention to the story. Think of effective punctuation as a self-effacing tool to aid your writing efficiency. Use it well.

And while we're at it, answer this: if you were a punctuation mark, which one would you be?

Tips in Action

Right now, write what you're grateful for and why:

- ____

- ____

- ____

- ____

- ____

- ____

- ____

- ____

- ____

- ____

58

"So You Think I Don't Appreciate You?" Gratitude Happens

A DEAR FRIEND recently challenged me about my mission statement. *Healing the world through teaching the power of gratitude.* "So," she said, "just how do you expect to do that?"

I explained that gratitude lifted people, that my own attitude of gratitude gave me a more compassionate viewpoint of life and hopefully let other people know how much they are valued. "I appreciate you," I added.

"Nonsense," she spouted out. "It's not enough to say *I love you* or *I appreciate you* without giving a reason why. It's too easy to say three little words and not mean them. How do I know you're not just trying to butter me up to get another dinner invitation?" Have I mentioned that she makes the most delicious lasagna you can imagine?

She was right, you know. One of my favorite columnists, Lisa Earle McLeod, recently wrote about how husbands never seem to feel appreciated, and wives don't want to thank them when they, the wives, feel unappreciated themselves. A vicious circle indeed.

Now what does this have to do with writing a novel or a short story? We want our characters to thrum with life energy. We want them to stand up in three dimensions and be accepted as real by our readers. We want our creations to be recognizable, don't we? I certainly do. So, why not create a gratitude list for our protagonist—and ones for the bad guys, too, just to be fair. Not just *I like you,* but *I like you and I'm willing to spend all this time writing you because . . .*

This is the kind of gratitude that helps us focus on why we feel connected to our characters. When we do that, we're more likely to write them in a way that will entrance our readers.

I like you because you act honorably.

I like you because you tell the truth.

Aw, put some gumption into it, Frannie.

Okay. I like you because when you lie, you do it with great gusto, and I end up laughing, or crying.

I like you because you act out the brat I'd like to be. *(Substitute a different b-word if you'd like.)*
I like you because I can depend on you to get into trouble whenever I need an interesting plot twist.
I like you because you let me explore a new world I didn't know existed before I started this writing.
I like you because you're ready to play with me at three in the morning when I get up to write because I can't sleep.

This is the kind of gratitude that works with sisters (real and imaginary):
I love you because you used to stand up for me on the playground.
I love you because even though you let me climb that tree that had the ants in it, you didn't laugh too much when I started howling.

This is the kind of gratitude that works with spouses (real, imaginary, current or former):
I love you because you taught me to change a flat tire.
I love you because you brush my hair without my asking.
I appreciate you because you helped me realize that I was 100% responsible for 50% of the problems in our marriage, and 50% responsible for 100% of the problems.

And this kind of gratitude works for editors, too:
I appreciate you because you hold me to the highest standards.
I appreciate you because you see my vision for these books of mine.

Try some gratitude today. Be specific. You may surprise yourself when you find out how many reasons there are to be grateful. Real thankfulness just might heal the world. And it might make your writing shine.

Tips in Action

Pick up a pigeon feather while you're out walking around. Pigeons are ubiquitous, so I doubt you'll have any trouble finding one, but you do have to walk outside, and you do have to look at the ground.

Cut off the end of the quill at an angle. Buy some kind of berries (or pick your own if you live in such an environment). Squash them. Dip quill into berry juice and see what happens.

Can you write with it? If not, laugh at yourself (and at me) and return to pencil or keyboard. Congratulate yourself on an experiment well-done.

59

Illuminated Manuscripts

I JUST FINISHED watching a video about illuminated manuscripts on National Public Radio's *Speaking of Faith* website. A monastic order in Wales commissioned a twentieth-century illuminated Bible, and this video followed the artist as he mixed his paints (starting with a fresh egg yolk) and cut his quill (starting with a fresh feather).

Although we don't produce illuminated manuscripts nowadays, I do hope that our manuscripts help to illuminate the mind, to bring puddles of light where murky misinformation once lurked. Illumination, after all, is not only the art of decorating a printed page, but is also the process of bringing light and clarity.

> *Use language the way an artist uses a brush (or a quill).*

One of the best ways to do this—besides starting with a clear concept of what we want to write about—is to use language the way an artist uses a brush (or a quill). It means selecting our words with care, layering the nuances in plotlines, and fleshing out our characters with subtle descriptions and believable dialogue.

How do we do these things? We study the work of other authors, gleaning ideas from each of them. We read how-to books and pay attention to the lessons therein. We attend classes that help us with areas where we need improvement. We listen to editors.

I'd like to recommend a book that lumps all four of these techniques into one easy-to-read reference. Chris Roerden wrote *Don't Murder Your Mystery.* She has collected hundreds of examples of fine writing that avoid the various no-no's such as shifty eyes, dying dialogue, toxic transcripts, and fatal flashbacks. She teaches us how to correct what she calls *wordiarrea,* how to break the description-first habit, how to prevent the slow death of a scene. Whether you write mysteries, historical novels, short stories, or chick lit, you need Chris Roerden's book.

Then cut your quill, mix your ink, and write with true illumination.

Tips in Action

Revising dialogue is one of those chores that will pay off in a big way.

Look through your latest manuscript and study the ways you show people talking with each other. Eliminate anything that even remotely sounds like my first example in this essay.

Now, show us how each person acts and reacts during the interplay. Letting their actions (rather than their thoughts) reflect their motivation will propel the story in a way that reiterations can simply never accomplish.

60

What Is It About the End of the Year?
Reiterations

THE FIRST THREE years I wrote this column, I wrote each December about resolutions for writers. The first list in 2004 was fairly straightforward: "I will write nothing but scintillating prose, if I can figure out how," for instance.

The next year showed a hint of where I was on my life journey: "I will write nothing but scintillating prose, if I can figure out how. Oh nonsense. Scintillating prose gets old fast if that's all there is. Good old short Anglo-Saxon words and simple straightforward sentences have a lot to be said for them. Forget the *scintillate* and go for *sense*."

In 2006 I threw it all to the wind and wrote about spaghetti. December of 2007 had me writing about children's books. I have no intention of going back to list resolutions ever again, unless I change my mind. Instead, I'd like to talk this year about reiterations.

> *Your words can sing like Vivaldi, stride like Rimski-Korsakov, exult like Mozart, croon like Sinatra, or holler like The Grateful Dead.*

To reiterate is more than simply to repeat. It is to do or say something over and over again with what Webster calls a *sometimes wearying effect.* Did you ever have that here-we-go-again feeling while reading an ineptly written dialogue?

"Bob, I want to go to the movies," Pam said.
"I hate movies," Bob responded.
"I know, but this one is special. I think you might like it," Pam argued.
"I hate movies," Bob replied.
"Okay, you win," Pam relented.

How long can this conversation seesaw back and forth before we throw the book in the trash? (Don't even *think* about donating such drivel to Goodwill.) It's not only the repetitive "I hate movies," but the way in which the attributions—said, responded, argued, replied, relented—march in strident mirror images of each other.

Let's try the same scene without the monotonous *reiterations*.

"Bob?" Pam slipped her shoes on. "I want to go to the movies."

He barely glanced at her. "I hate movies."
"I know, but this one is special. I think you might like it."
"I . . . hate . . . movies." Bob ground out the words.
Pam took off one shoe and threw it against the closet. "Okay," she shouted. "You win."

I've written before about the possibilities inherent in attributions, as well as the rhythm of language as a way to make your writing more distinctive. This month, take any dialogue you've written and plot the way you use *said*, or any other word that denotes who's speaking. Then fiddle with varying the rhythm of the lines. Your words can sing like Vivaldi, stride like Rimski-Korsakov, exult like Mozart, croon like Sinatra, or holler like The Grateful Dead. Choose the kind of music you want to make, and play on. It's a great way to end the year.

Tips in Action

Go to the library (again).

- Pick out a non-fiction book that isn't something you'd normally read. Read it. Jot down the impulses it generates. How could what you've read add richness to your fiction?

- After you've done that, write a hundred words about what you believe. Send me what you've come up with. I'd love to hear from you. fran@franstewart.com

61

NPR—New Possibilities, Really

WHEN DID *I'm happy to help you* turn into *no problem*? By the same token, *you're welcome* and *of course I will* have both devolved into that same word duo. I can't blame it on the text-messaging generation with their *brb* for *be right back* or *lol* for *lots of laughs*, or is that supposed to be *lots of love*? Perhaps *lol* is contextual; laughs after a joke or snide comment and love as a closing. No, the *no problem* problem began before blackberries became ubiquitous. It seems to be the same sort of downward evolution taken by *I love you*, which so often now we see or hear with no first person evident.

I subscribe to Garrison Keillor's *The Writers Almanac*. I try to listen to him on NPR each day, but if I miss hearing it, I still receive an email giving me a poem and a listing of noted authors born on that day. Last January, on the 14th, to be precise, Garrison told me that the Chinese-born writer Anchee Min, who learned English at age twenty-seven by watching *Sesame Street* and *Oprah,* once said her writing process was "like a long line of ants walking for blocks

> *I'm reading* Stiff: the curious lives of human cadavers. ***It's a surprisingly funny book.***

carrying one crooked cricket leg." To this comment, are we supposed to reply, *no problem, Anchee?* Shouldn't we rather read her memoir, *Red Azalea*, and marvel at how that cricket-bearing process brought one exquisite word after another to the printed page, and then try to learn something from her that will improve our own writing?

I find out about a lot of good books on National Public Radio. Right now, besides reading oodles of murder mysteries as a preparation for my internet radio show, I'm reading *Stiff: the curious lives of human cadavers*. It's a fascinating and surprisingly funny book. Robert Siegel interviewed the author, Mary Roach, on NPR's *All Things Considered* about five years ago. I noted the title on my "Read Someday" list and finally got around to it.

Now, if you haven't read *This I Believe: the personal philosophies of remarkable men and women,* then you're missing a rich well of ideas to fertilize your own writing and your own life. The concept began with Edward R. Murrow in the 1950s and continues today. The editorial team for this volume, led by Jay Allison and Dan Gediman, asked people—all sorts

of people—to "write a few hundred words expressing the core principles that guide your life—your personal credo." Thousands of people answered that call, writing their words and recording them for use on public radio. I did the writing part of the assignment. You can read my credo on my website at http://www.franstewart.com/fran.htm. I went well beyond the "few hundred" stricture, I'll admit, but the experience was a defining moment in my life. I strongly suggest that you participate in this exercise as well.

Just think, we could change *no problem* to *New Possibilities*. Really.

Tips in Action

Have you written anything about shadows in your current manuscript? Or ever, for that matter?

If not, look through your story and see where shadows could add the right touch. You can make them friendly, threatening, murky, delicate, incisive. You choose. Just be sure that they reflect the right mood.

62

Shadow-Play

LET'S LOOK AT shadows. They play—or can play—a wide range of parts in our writing. Shadows set tone, obviously, but they can be equally effective as timing devices and descriptive ploys, not just for landscapes but for faces as well.

I recall years ago sketching the face of a woman who sat across from me in an airport lounge. I've never claimed to be an artist, but sometimes I like to try. Seldom do I share the results with anyone except my cats. They promised long ago not to laugh at me. On this occasion, though, I showed the drawing to my sister, who *is* an artist. "You drew the shadows," she said, "and left out the lines along the side of her face." That was because the woman had sat in a shaft of sunlight that erased any distinction between the curve of her cheek and the wall behind her. I couldn't *see* a line there, so I didn't draw one.

> *My inexpert shadows turned her into an enigma.*

Instead I drew the shadows beneath her angular cheek bone and the jut of her chin, around her eye and beside her nose. My sister was impressed. It's the only time she's *ever* been impressed by one of my sketches. I wish I'd saved the sketch, just as I wish I'd saved a lot of my early essays and stories, but the memory of those shadows on that woman's face still haunts me. I may have managed the shadows, but I didn't draw her well enough. I didn't capture her essence. My art lies in words, and while the pencil drawing may have been technically interesting, it stopped short of capturing who that woman truly was.

My inexpert shadows turned her into an enigma. Did the sunlight that day come from a bright spring morning or a harsh mid-summer? Was the woman an undercover agent, a jilted lover, a harried executive, a wilted mom (or stepmom)? Was she headed out or headed home? Was she someone's best friend, or a harpy-like harridan who had just sent the emotionally unstable protagonist spinning back into an alcoholic dead end? Had she inherited those deep-set eyes from her paternal grandmother or were they a reflection of her inner turmoil? Was her angular cheekbone the result of ethnicity or anorexia? If she had raised her hand, would it have blocked the light and created a dark slash of a shadow, or would the light have penetrated between her fingers and outlined each one in an unearthly red glow, like a flashlight beneath a blanket in the middle of the night?

Shadows. Sometimes they ask more questions than they answer. Unless we know how to sketch them with a deft pen.

Tips in Action

Everyone has seen something die. Choose a death you've witnessed and write about it.

So what if it was an ant you stepped on. No matter if it was a chipmunk your dog brought to you, or a lump of roadkill struck by the truck in front of you.

Write the death from two different viewpoints (yours and the ant's or the dog's or the trucker's). Which scenario was the most effective? What feelings did writing about the death from a viewpoint other than your own bring up in you that seeing the death may not have evoked?

63

Seven Years—Reflections on Death

AS I WRITE this in March for an April publication date, it has been seven years since my father died. On this day seven years ago, I sat at his bedside and watched as he walked down that final staircase, step by step. I heard his breathing get shallower and slower. I even timed it, watching the second hand sweep around the big gold watch he'd worn for years, the watch that now hung limp on his skeletal wrist, the watch I put on my own wrist after he died, and wear it still.

He'd stopped eating three days before, a common occurrence as someone approaches death and the various bodily systems begin to shut down. Still, when my niece brought her mom and me a popsicle to split, our dad looked at it and grinned. "Do you want some?" my sister asked, and he nodded. She lifted her half carefully up to his lips, and he licked it a few times, then settled back, fully aware that grape popsicle would be the last flavor he ever tasted. A little while later, he greeted and talked with someone neither I nor my sister could see, and the joy that radiated from him was palpable.

> *Call it wisdom, if you will. Or just say I'm an old fart with lots of memories.*

Now what does this have to do with writing? At that time, I had just begun writing ORANGE AS MARMALADE, my first mystery. It took me until this past year before I wrote my father's death into one of my books. I wanted people to know that death can be gentle, and that it's nothing to fear. So I wrote the death of Wallace Masters, one of the minor characters in my series, early in INDIGO AS AN IRIS. It wasn't a murder. It was a natural death. It was my father's death, although I left out the popsicle and the watch. The murder came later in the book.

I belong to Sisters in Crime, and recently in their members' group posts, people have been talking about the joys of being a *Late Bloomer*. When we wait awhile before we start to write, or at least before we try to get published, we have so many more life experiences to draw on, and therefore, much more of value to say. Call it wisdom, if you will. Or just say I'm an old fart with lots of memories. Whatever. But I'm brave enough now to write a death and show its meaning. I'm brave enough to lay bare a part of my soul.

Enough of this. I'm off to buy a grape popsicle and celebrate life.

Tips in Action

Think about what you're writing now. Does it follow a particular formula? If so, write down the steps in that formula.

If not, jot down some ways in which you could revise it so that your end result might be more publishable.

64

Writing to Formula – Curse or Blessing?

RECENTLY ON MY internet radio show, *Mystery Matters: Where Murder is an Open Book*, I spoke with Claire Matturro, author of the Lilly Belle Cleary mysteries, and asked her if she had any advice for would-be mystery writers. Now, keep in mind that anyone can write a mystery. The trick is to write one that's publishable. Claire suggested that one read good, successful mysteries. "Study the plot lines," she said, "and figure out what the formula is."

Formula? Aargh! Isn't that a dirty word? Well, no, according to Claire. Let's think about that. We disparage an author who "writes to formula." What do we mean by that? Well, the plot line gets so blinkin' predictable and the dialogue so stilted that each successive book in the series is, quite frankly, boring. That can happen after one's written fifteen books with the same characters. Or it can occur in the first book.

> *Formula? Aargh! Isn't that a dirty word?*

That boring predictability, though, is not what Claire was talking about. Think back to a college term paper or a physics experiment. State the problem; state what you're going to do about it; state how you did it; state how the action led to the final result; wrap it up. Is that a formula? Yes. Now think about a mystery—any mystery. Introduce problem (like a dead body); show characters (preferably through dialogue and action rather than through description); show relationship between characters, ideally as they work though the problem; introduce a bigger problem that besets the main character (may be self-induced or come from an outside source); resolve the problem as the solution is revealed. Is that a formula? Yes.

One thing I've seen, though, as I've read two to five books a week preparing for the Friday morning live interviews, is that the formula works, and the infinite variety of ways in which the formula can be manipulated to fit each author's particular voice is fascinating. I never thought I'd recommend writing to formula, but now that Claire opened my eyes to a new way of looking at it, I'll say, "Go for it." Use that formula, but use it well. I'd love to read the result.

Tips in Action

What was your most memorable communication in five words?

Why was it memorable?

65

Five Words or Fewer

SEVERAL WEEKS AGO, John Lemley on WABE's *City Café* asked Public Radio listeners to call in and tell the most important words they ever received in some form of communication. The limitation, though, was that it had to be "five words or less." Grrr! Miss Johnson, my 7th grade English teacher would be grinding her teeth if she were still alive to do so. I can still hear her pontificating about the difference between *fewer* and *less.* "Use the former word if what it's describing can be counted. Use the latter if you're talking about something that can be measured." Fewer boulders on this beach and less sand on that one, for instance. Fewer people at a concert generate less volume in their applause. Fewer birds would mean less birdsong in the morning—awful thought.

That being said, what would be the most important five (or fewer) words I ever heard? Well, I'd have to mention two sets of five, and both of them involved one particular person. The first was in November of 1974. It was "Your pregnancy test was positive." Since this was a planned and much-anticipated pregnancy, I floated down the stairs of the Planned Parenthood Clinic in Burlington, Vermont, grinning my fool head off.

> *"I helped carry bodies yesterday."*

Several years ago my son, the end result of that pregnancy, went on vacation to Dahab, Egypt, to scuba dive. When three bombs exploded in a crowded marketplace, the Egyptian government immediately shut down all internet and phone service. I spent a frantic day and a half, searching the news reports, hoping and praying, remembering how willingly I had taken on the role of mother, and how much light my son spread around him. I remembered reading him *Lord of the Rings* when he was in first grade. I remembered trips to the Shakespeare Tavern with him once he was grown. I tried very hard not to go into fear mode, but the best five words I ever read—bittersweet, but still the best—were "I helped carry bodies yesterday."

I'd urge you to think of five words (or fewer) that have meant the world to you. If you're writing a novel, I'd suggest that you might want to use this as an exercise to get closer to your protagonist (or a minor character who isn't well-formed yet). What would she say if she had to deliver a shocking message? How would he introduce a litany of hope? What five words (or fewer) would cause their hearts to leap up, like Wordsworth's at the sight of his rainbow?

And, to encourage you in this exercise, all I can say is, "Sure, you can do it."

Tips in Action

Consider these seven words: *anticipation, dread, cynicism, bewilderment, willingness, doubt, exhilaration.* Apply each of these to your protagonist's view of an upcoming meeting, phone call, or wedding—whatever event would fit into your plotline.

Could you revise that scene to bring in more emotion? Would the scene benefit from a change of pace?

66

Panting or Sighing – A Lesson from the Breath

DID YOU KNOW that the process that regulates your breathing is subject to whimsy? We can control how we breathe or we can simply let our bodies remember to do it for us. Some muscles are voluntary—crook your index finger and you'll see what I mean—while some are involuntary. Try to rearrange the speed at which you digest that carrot you just ate. Breathe fast. Breathe more slowly. That's voluntary. Now, think about what your breath has been doing the other 23.997 hours of this day. That's involuntary.

We writers can learn from our breathing. The lesson is called pacing. If we choose to write a fun, light, breezy story, one that would classify as a "beach read," the pace will be totally different than a thought-provoking tale that delves into the intricacy of our relationships. In the first case, our pacing will probably stay light or brisk, the way our breath is on a gentle walk. In the second case, though, we'll have to shift to abdominal breathing, drawing the story deep into our lungs and expelling it slowly. You might even gasp it out the way you would struggle for oxygen if you ran a forced marathon, but that's not the kind of book I write.

> **Learn to trust the process. You can always rewrite if you need to.**

Does that mean you have to yoga-breathe for 75,000 words? Of course not. As you plot your story arc, be sure to regulate your pacing. Insert some breathing spaces into your thriller or some tension into your beach read. Too much meat can be just as unhealthy as too much ice cream.

Word choice is one of the tools you can use to set the pace. Consider these seven words: *anticipation, dread, cynicism, bewilderment, willingness, doubt, exhilaration.* Apply each of these to your protagonist's view of an upcoming meeting, phone call, or wedding. See how the pace slows with some and speeds up with others?

When you're rewriting, pay attention to your own breath. Does one chapter elicit an anticipatory breath pattern or does it slow your breath into a deliberate susurration? Look at your minor characters. They're a good device for varying the pace. A well-placed and well-

delineated walk-on character can add anything from laughter to despair. At the same time, remember to imbue your protagonist with both light and dark moments. If you want to bore your reader, create a hero who makes all the right choices all the time. Or a heroine who makes all the wrong ones. Stereotypical characters will propel readers into mind-numbing ho-humming, hardly a worthy goal for a writer.

Be open to the sudden intake of breath when a character you thought you knew heads off on a tangent. Follow along, whether huffing and puffing or with bated breath. Learn to trust the process. You can always rewrite if you need to.

Here's one more tip. Use colored markers in the margins of your latest draft. Red for fast-paced paragraphs, orange for slowing or shifting ones, and green for slow. Try yellow for humor and blue for a darker mood. Next, flip quickly through the pages and see which color predominates. You can also do this on the computer, highlighting the various sections in bright colors. Then scroll down quickly, noting the colors as you go.

Remember, you are the author. Your characters may dictate entire chapters, yet you have not only the right but the ultimate responsibility as well, to determine the pacing of your novel. Inhale, exhale. We have to do both in order to live.

Tips in Action

I've already done *up* and *down*. Now you do *right* and *left*. Or *in* and *out*.

67

Ups and Downs – Situational Directions

IF WE WOLF it down, we might eventually have to throw it up. My granddog came for a visit recently, gorged on a patch of particularly succulent grass, and . . . well, you get the idea. It started me thinking, though, about the way we use directional words like **up** and **down**. Phrases like *drink it down* and *barf it up* are fairly logical. So are *rev up* and *power down*, if one thinks of the sound pitches involved in these two processes, but when I searched for other examples, I found that there didn't seem to be any rules.

In order to *look down your nose*, you might very well need to lift your chin, for instance. And why would we *look up* a word in the dictionary, when we'd probably need to lower our heads—or at least our eyes—in order to do that? We *send down* murderers when we incarcerate them, and *put down* ailing animals when we euthanize them. Yet we *hang up* a phone, which has nothing to do with the movement involved, and we get down on the floor to do *push-ups*, and then stand up and walk around in order to *cool down*.

> *My granddog came for a visit recently, gorged on a patch of particularly succulent grass, and . . . well, you get the idea.*

There are *pop-ups* on the computer screen, as well as *drop-down menus,* yet an actor who wants to get back at a fellow player will *upstage* him, while an irate employer will *dress down* an employee. That same employer might, however, approve an official *dress-down day,* thereby delighting that employee.

When we get tired, we *run down*, a reference to watches that had to be *wound up* each day so they wouldn't *run down*. In an increasingly digital age, will that phrase become obsolete—what, after all, does *clockwise* mean to the average child today? I doubt it, since we frequently insist on running around and running ourselves ragged while we *run up* phone bills trying to *run down* information we need to *update*. And we get *uptight* in the process, possibly enough to create an *uproar*, or at the very least an *upset*.

We may be *upbeat* until someone *upbraids* us. We *update* a friend by giving them a *rundown* of our day. If we want to *upgrade* to more fuel efficiency, we may need to *downsize* our vehicle. Did you ever want to *upholster* your couch in a *down* comforter? Ever put money

down on a house? Ever had to *ante-up* in a poker game? Cities may be slow on the *uptake* to revitalize their *downtown* areas.

People in Vermont go *down east* to get to Maine. People from Maine go *up* to Boston. And why, I ask you, are the hills in England called the *downs*? Hmm. I need to stop this roller-coaster ride. I'm not ready to go anywhere in my *pickup* truck, and I don't want to play *pickup* sticks. I'm not interested in a *pickup* at a dance club; I'd rather *pick up* on the nuances of good conversation. That's it! I'll *pick up* the phone, *ring up* a friend, and *count down* the time until we can *scrape up* the money for a dinner *uptown*. Of course, if my friend lived on the side of the hill below me, I'd have to *ring down* to that friend. Maybe I'll just *turn up* the radio and *dance up a storm*.

Tips in Action

What has been your experience with war? It could be combat on a national scale or a bitter personal rivalry from yesterday or from years ago.

Go deep within and write what comes up.

68

Visions of War

I THINK IT was in 1992 that a friend gave me a copy of a book of poetry written by women who had served in the Vietnam War. *Visions of War; Dreams of Peace* was the memorable title. I inhaled that book. A few of the poems were obviously amateur, but all of them were moving. Some of the poems tore at my heartstrings; some of them tore at my gut. The book had been the brainchild of Lynda Van Devanter and Joan A. Furey, both of them accomplished poets in their own right.

I've returned to that book over the years, particularly each time this country was led into yet another heartbreaking military conflict. As the authors say in their preface, "We believe the poems and thoughts in this book have great value beyond their literary quality. They help people to understand the reality of war from a perspective rarely seen or acknowledged."

If you could do anything you wanted to (and you can!), would writing be high on the list or at the bottom of the barrel?

Keep that in mind.

Yesterday I received an email from Sharon Wildwind, a woman I'd never heard of, praising my internet radio show **Mystery Matters**. I emailed back saying that I had checked out her website and noticed that she had served in Vietnam. "Have you by any chance," I wrote, "ever read *Visions of War; Dreams of Peace?* It's a collection of poems written by women who served there. I came across it years ago and was so incredibly moved.*"*

Not only had she heard of it, some of her poems, written under an earlier name, were in it. So I asked if she'd like me to send her my margin notes on her poems. We ended up having quite an email discussion.

My point? It's now seventeen years since I first read that book. Because the perspective showed "a reality of war . . . rarely seen or acknowledged," it stayed with me and sparked a vital connection almost two decades later.

Do we take our written words for granted or do we ever wonder if people will dwell on them and make margin notes? Will they read our books, poems, stories years from now? Please understand that I am not suggesting that we attempt to write dreadfully meaningful works for the illumination of either present or future audiences. Such efforts on our part tend to result in boring, preachy tomes. Still, as we rewrite and revise, let's keep in mind that—if our works do happily last—we'll want to be proud of them even if/when we grow beyond them.

Why do you write? What's in it for you? If you could do anything you wanted to (and you can!), would writing be high on the list or at the bottom of the barrel? If it's at the bottom, I suggest that you become a dedicated reader. If it's up there at the top, go for it!

Oh dear. I've just broken my rule of only one exclamation point allowed.

Tips in Action

Today, do something irrepressibly messy. Then write about it—why you chose it, how you did it, how you felt, what came of it.

69

Confessions of a Time Saver – the Toothbrush Writing Model

Warning: read this between meals if you're squeamish.

OKAY. I HAVE a confession to make. I find that I can save a lot of time if I brush my teeth in the shower. Think about it. There need be absolutely no concern over where the spit is going to land. Splashing is allowed, even encouraged. So what if I gargle and it spills over? When the shower is complete, I dry off and become respectable again.

I write the same way, and I certainly hope you'll try it out. The process is called First Draft, Revise/Rewrite, Final Draft, Final Revision. Whew! Worrying about your first draft is like fussing if the toothpaste drops off the brush into the sink. Sure it's hard to clean up, especially if it dries before you notice it. Big deal. Write your first draft as if you were standing in the shower and let the splashing, the fun, bubble over. The clean-up will be a breeze, I promise you.

> *There need be absolutely no concern over where the spit is going to land.*

Your dentist may have told you to start with the right upper molars and work your way methodically around the upper teeth, then repeat the process with your lower teeth. Baloney-feathers. Start wherever you want. Sometimes the first chapter I write is one that I know will come toward the end of the book. If you're a methodical writer—chapter two is written *after* chapter one—okay. But splashing around a bit might free up your manuscript. It's worth a try.

Revision is like rinsing out your mouth. Now is the time to wash away the leftover toothpaste. It should be pretty obvious what is extraneous, particularly if you've been reading this column for any length of time. Look for excessive adverbs, boring descriptions, lengthy backstory. Clear them out, the way you would those leftover bubbles on your chin. Is your timeline concise? Is the setting clear enough? Is each character fully dimensional? Did you buy old-fashioned toothpowder when you really wanted mint gel? Put the changes on your shopping list.

Now where does the flossing come in? Well, yes, I do that in the shower also. It saves me from the icky feeling of all that saliva dribbling down my arm, and I never have to clean speckles off the mirror. Stephen King said that you need to get to the point (I'm paraphrasing obviously) where you're deleting perfectly good passages, since you (hopefully) eliminated all the bad ones in previous revisions. The goal is to take teeth that look perfectly clean by now and clean them up even more. Get into those hollows and fissures. Look at every scene, every set of dialogue, every aspect of each character. Are they true? Are they clean? Is there any lurking discrepancy that you can root out, like a popcorn hull that somehow cemented itself to the back of your first molar?

The final rewrite is like gargling. Inject some of those missing elements the book needs to bring it alive, to freshen up the story line. It can be sweet-tasting or astringent, with essence of lemon or cinnamon. Decide what's right for your mouth, and your book.

Brush, floss, gargle, and send it into the world—clean, well-dressed, and ready to thrive. Don't forget to smile.

Tips in Action

What esoteric part of life are you interested in?

Maybe you're drawn to snorkeling or cave-diving, ancient manuscripts or 17th century France, the Pony Express or early telegraphy, miniature doll houses or architectural drawings of skyscrapers. Have you used your knowledge of that field in your writing? Is there a way you could introduce bits of it here and there in the book you're working on now?

Jot down some ideas and see where they lead you.

70

Esoterica –
The Art of Explaining Speciality Items

OVER THE PAST number of months, I've shared with several of my friends my decision to end **Mystery Matters**, my internet radio show, at the end of this year. Lyn Hammond Gray, my friend who wrote her doctoral dissertation on *Stellar Psychology*, told me, "Well of course. You're a Capricorn with Libra rising." Now, that may mean something to you, but it certainly didn't illuminate anything for me.

Then, another friend, whose interests lie in numerology, said, "Well, of course. You're an eight." I am? Wish I knew what that meant.

> *Jeri bought the biggest slab of meat she could carry, nailed it to her son's swing set (he was at school), and proceeded to experiment with great vigor.*

Now comes the question I keep asking in this column: what does this have to do with writing? Any time we write about esoteric ideas—ones that our readers might not understand readily—it is our duty to explain ourselves so that any basically intelligent reader can grasp whatever we're dealing with, whether it be something in the setting, the action, the dialogue, or the backstory.

The challenge is to give the information without sounding preachy, boringly erudite, or downright haughty. How to do this? Well, it certainly helps if we have our facts straight. Research for a novel can be great fun. I interviewed Jeri Westerson, author of the Crispin Guest medieval noirs, in September. She told me she'd wanted to know what it felt like to stab someone with a sword. None of her friends would volunteer, and she couldn't very well ask her protagonist—he lives in 14th century London.

Jeri bought the biggest slab of meat she could carry, nailed it to her son's swing set (he was at school), and proceeded to experiment with great vigor. Did I mention she happens to own a fine sword and several daggers? Listen to the interview to learn how she disposed of the body once she'd finished hacking at it. When I read a Jeri Westerson book, I feel sure that Crispin's experiences are "real," because of the subtle way Jeri works that esoteric information into the mystery.

That leads me to the second point: Don't *tell*. Do *show*. If you're writing someone who is adept at numerology or the tarot or listening to the voices of dead people—all experiences that many of us might not be familiar with—please don't lay out three paragraphs of explanation. Put your character into a situation that involves that particular art and show her working her way through it. You can use comments, questions, or even sarcasm from other characters to further your reader's understanding.

My newest book, *A Slaying Song Tonight* will be a departure from my Biscuit McKee mystery series. It's a dark story revolving around a serial killer in the Midwest who begins her killing in December of 1892 and is finally caught—forty Christmases and thirteen bodies later—in December of 1931. What, you may ask, is esoteric about that? Well, serial killings for one, and courtroom scenes for another. Then add in the historical element. For research I attended an aggravated assault trial; plowed through dusty, fragile archives of court cases from 1880 to 1940; contacted seemingly ancient ranchers and farmers who knew such things as whether or not their grandparents had screen doors in 1892. This research was not as hair-raising perhaps as stabbing a slab of meat, but still satisfying in its own way. Then there were the internet forays to find out when *Jingle Bells* was written (1857, early enough to be my killer's favorite song).

I've been saying for six years in these columns that it's important for writers to stretch their wings. Well, this stretch, particularly the wicked plot twist halfway through the book, put my wings to the test indeed. But why would I depart so *drastically* from my cozy Biscuit McKee mystery series? Well, naturally I would. I think about something for quite awhile but then act very quickly, because I'm a Capricorn. And I always look for balance; it's that Libra rising thing. Then again, I'm an eight. When I find out what that means, I'll let you know.

Tips in Action

Write a succinct paragraph that evokes your passion for life. If you can't think what that passion is, begin now to investigate the possibilities.

List ways in which you could enrich your experience. Ignite a flame and follow that light.

71

Start Where You Are - Bel Canto Flute

FOR THE PAST year, I've read two to five mysteries each week in order to be able to carry on an intelligible and intelligent conversation with my weekly guests on *Mystery Matters*. Fortunately, I've managed to read a few other books as well. The most recent is *Bel Canto Flute: the Rampal School* by Sheryl Cohen. This non-fiction account chronicles her thirty years of study and friendship with Jean-Pierre Rampal. One of Cohen's admonitions to her own flute students is: "Every day, start where you are" (p. 29). Good advice, indeed. I was delighted when Cohen went on to quote Basho, the 17th-century Japanese poet, although I prefer this slightly different translation of his haiku:

> *Ida described her brother-in-law Kelvin as "an absolute zero of a man."*

> Seek not to tread in
> the Masters' footsteps. Instead,
> seek what they all sought.

Maybe it's that end-of-the-year reckoning that's moving me to such reflections, but I see a great deal of sense here for writers. Several months ago I found a mystery, whose author will remain nameless. I could almost see his instruction book close at hand: "Spice up your writing with similes," the manual must have said. "I'll put in three per paragraph," said the author. "Be sure to include humor," said the manual. "Jokes! Lots of jokes," said the author. "Avoid predictability," said the manual. "Whee! Look at all these plot twists," said the author, who then wrote one of the most ludicrously convoluted stories I've ever encountered, a clear case of following in the Masters' footsteps without looking for the greater vision.

Have you ever studied a bar of the mineral selenite? This crystalline form of gypsum often forms perfectly straight milky white layers. Those easily discernible layers are the basis for selenite's place in the metaphysical hierarchy as a representative of Truth. Whether your writing is fiction or non-fiction, serious, humorous, light, dark, or somewhere in between, if you don't have straight layers of Truth in there somewhere, you're missing the boat. If you fail to seek what the masters sought, you're not likely to hold my interest. And if, every day, you do not start where you are, you may find yourself lost in a swamp of misunderstanding and misplaced dreams, like an otter that is transported to a desert with nary a stream in sight.

I acknowledge that you may enjoy the three laughs per minute approach of our unnamed author. I'd rather read (and write) a more subtle, organic sort of humor. In my third mystery, GREEN AS A GARDEN HOSE, for instance, I have Ida describe her brother-in-law Kelvin as "an absolute zero of a man." If you don't get it, that's okay. If you *do*, however, you glimpse one of those layers of truth and humor that adds richness to the printed page.

Cohen quotes Rampal as saying, "The flute is just a pipe, like a paintbrush is to an artist. Why would anyone think of a paintbrush when looking at a painting?" (p.10). When we force our instrument—our words, when we follow instructions diligently but lose sight of the joy that could suffuse those words, we produce art that is nothing but painfully obvious brushstrokes. This year, let's agree to seek what the Masters sought, to infuse our writing with the passion and the truth that drives us, and to start—every single day—right where we are.

The music begins now.

Tips in Action

Plan a surprise party for your protagonist.

- Who would you invite?

- How would they interact?

- Where would you hold it?

- What would you serve?

- Who would eat the food, and who would abstain?

- How would the weather affect the party?

- What would the conversation convey?

- Would your honored guest be delighted, angry, confused, mortified?

- And how did you feel once the party was over?

72

Come to My Party

YESTERDAY I HOSTED an open house for my sister Diana Alishouse, who's visiting me from Colorado, so I could introduce a lot of people to her new book, *Depression Visible: the Ragged Edge*. This morning I got to thinking about how an open house relates to our experiences as writers.

I have cats who prefer to be reclusive until they make up their minds about new people, so I chose to sequester them during the party. In my books, some of my characters have secrets (doesn't everyone?), areas of their lives they choose to keep private, and I reveal those secrets only when they're pertinent to the plot. Yesterday, for instance, one person asked to see the cats, so I took her upstairs for a private viewing, although one cat stayed burrowed under the comforter. Give your readers glimpses by building your plots carefully so the secrets don't spill out all at once.

> *M&Ms in a pretty bowl? Sure. Cream cheese smothered in hot pepper jelly? Of course. (It was the hit of the party, by the way.) Chicken wings? Too messy.*

Deciding how to unveil those revelations is a bit like putting together the shopping list before the party. M&Ms in a pretty bowl? Sure. Cream cheese smothered in hot pepper jelly? Of course. (It was the hit of the party, by the way.) Chicken wings? Too messy. And so on. Sometimes, though, a guest will appear bringing a gift of food to share. Find a bowl for that trail mix and see how it goes. If nobody eats it, you'll have leftovers. If a plot element doesn't seem to work, either throw it out or try using it in your next book.

My mystery series has a lot of characters, rather like the extensive list of people I invited to the party. I'd better think about how my guests might interact, and be sure that people get more than a cursory introduction. Mozelle is an artist that I know through the National League of American Pen Women. Mozelle, this is Nancy, who is a tenor in the Gwinnett Choral Guild. After a few more comments I can leave them, fairly certain that their conversation will lead them to some common ground. Likewise, the characters in our books show most clearly through their dialogue. Put them together and let them talk about something that is interesting to them both. Or something that one is passionate about and

the other is antagonistic toward. It's up to you to introduce your characters effectively. Be sure that somehow or other you let your readers come to understand their motivations, their passions.

Getting our houses ready for a party is somewhat akin to creating the setting of our books. Whoops! That means I'd better clean my *whole* house, since people will be roaming all over, looking for the toilet but glancing into other rooms as they walk past. If you can't draw a map of the place where your story is set, you may be missing the boat. That doesn't mean you have to put a map in your book, but you need that map in your head, and then you need to translate it onto the pages so your readers will feel they could walk along the streets or canoe down the river you've put before them. You might want to reread Essay #33.

The purpose of my party (the plot) was to let people meet my sister and buy an autographed copy of her book. But books without interesting subplots are boring. I had several tables (subplots) set up in my family room where my guests could work on putting together a jigsaw puzzle of Biscuit McKee's attic (maybe I'll explain that in one of my future columns) or they could decorate rocks. Yes. That's what I said. My granddaughter and I took dozens of smooth, fairly flat rocks several weeks ago and painted them white on the top surface. I spread all of them on a table along with two dozen or so bright-colored markers. Amazing what people came up with. And you should have heard the conversations that sprang up as people drew stars and arrows and words and pictures. Meanwhile, the talk around the jigsaw table started out with "We need to find all the straight-edged border pieces," but soon spread to a networking meeting—"Stellar psychology? What's that?" In my own books, I've used subplots to introduce my readers to suicide prevention, bipolar disorder, green funerals, ethical treatment of animals, and organic gardening. So, in your own writing, set up those tables, put your characters there, introduce a few new guests, and see what happens.

Remember to invite me to your next open house. I'd love to meet you and your friends.

Index

Index

Index